Mathematics

Peter Sherran

Core 7

CAMBRIDGE
UNIVERSITY PRESS

CAMBRIDGE UNIVERSITY PRESS
Cambridge, New York, Melbourne, Madrid, Cape Town, Singapore, São Paulo, Delhi

Cambridge University Press
The Edinburgh Building, Cambridge CB2 8RU, UK

www.cambridge.org
Information on this title: www.cambridge.org/9780521722247

© Cambridge University Press 2008

First published 2008

Book printed in the United Kingdom at the University Press, Cambridge

A catalogue record for this publication is available from the British Library

ISBN 978-0-521-72224-7 paperback with CD-ROM

Contents

Introduction

Take advantage of the pupil CD

Cambridge Essentials Mathematics comes with a pupil CD in the back. This contains the entire book as an interactive PDF file, which you can read on your computer using free Adobe Reader software from Adobe (www.adobe.com/products/acrobat/readstep2.html). As well as the material you can see in the book, the PDF file gives you extras when you click on the buttons you will see on most pages; see the inside front cover for a brief explanation of these.

To use the CD, simply insert it into the CD or DVD drive of your computer. You will be prompted to install the contents of the CD to your hard drive. Installing will make it easier to use the PDF file, because the installer creates an icon on your desktop that launches the PDF directly. However, it will run just as well straight from the CD.

If you want to install the contents of the disc onto your hard disc yourself, this is easily done. Just open the disc contents in your file manager (for Apple Macs, double click on the CD icon on your desktop; for Windows, open My Computer and double click on your CD drive icon), select all the files and folders and copy them wherever you want.

Take advantage of the teacher CD

The *Teacher Material* CD-ROM for *Cambridge Essentials Mathematics* contains enhanced interactive PDFs. As well as all the features of the pupil PDF, teachers also have access to e-learning materials and links to the *Essentials Mathematics* Planner – a new website with a full lesson planning tool, including worksheets, homeworks, assessment materials, guidance and example lesson plans. The e-learning materials are also fully integrated into the Planner, letting you see the animations in context and alongside all the other materials.

Sequences

- Using symbols to represent numbers
- Increasing and decreasing sequences
- How to use a term–to–term rule
- How to use a position–to–term rule

Keywords

You should know

explanation 1

1 Each symbol stands for a number. What is each number?

a $\triangle + 3 = 5$ b $\star - 6 = 4$ c $\hexagon \times 2 = 8$ d $3 + \diamond = 15$

e $9 - \heartsuit = 2$ f $5 \times \blacksquare = 55$ g $\blacktriangledown \div 3 = 4$ h $\diamondsuit \div 10 = 3$

i $11 - \blacktriangleleft = 3$ j $14 + \clubsuit = 21$ k $\blacktriangleright + \blacktriangleright = 10$ l $\ast + \ast + \ast = 60$

2 $\blacktriangle = 7$ and $\bullet = 5$. Find the value of these expressions.

a $\blacktriangle + 2$ b $2 \times \blacktriangle$ c $\blacktriangle - 4$ d $3 + \blacktriangle$

e $\bullet + 6$ f $10 - \bullet$ g $3 \times \bullet$ h $\bullet - 4$

i $\blacktriangle + \bullet$ j $\blacktriangle - \bullet$ k $\bullet \times \blacktriangle$ l $\blacktriangle \times \blacktriangle$

m $\bullet \times \bullet$ n $\bullet \div \bullet$ o $\blacktriangle \div \blacktriangle$ p $\blacktriangle + \bullet + 6$

3 $\star = 6$ and $\spadesuit = 8$. Find the value of these expressions.

a $\star + \star$ b $2 \times \star$ c $\spadesuit + \spadesuit$ d $2 \times \spadesuit$

e $\spadesuit + \spadesuit + \spadesuit$ f $3 \times \spadesuit$ g $\star + \star + \star$ h $3 \times \star$

4 Repeat question 3 using $\star = 10$ and $\spadesuit = 4$.

Write down anything that you notice about your answers.

5 $\ast = 9$. Find a quick way to work this out.
$\ast + \ast + \ast + \ast + \ast + \ast + \ast + \ast + \ast + \ast$
Explain how you got your answer.

6 ♥ = 20. Write the value of each of these.

    a 4 more than ♥   **b** twice ♥   **c** 3 less than ♥

    d half of ♥   **e** ♥ less than 31   **f** ♥ more than 4

    g 5 times ♥   **h** ♥ more than ♥

7 Repeat question **6**, using ♥ = 24. Which of the answers is smaller when ♥ = 24 than when ♥ = 20?

8 ★ + △ = 5. Write down three pairs of values of ★ and △.

explanation 2

9 Copy and complete the table. One has been done for you.

	Start number	Change	Result
	3	Increase by 5	3 + 5 = 8
a	7	Increase by 11	
b	12		12 + 6 = 18
c		Increase by 10	21 + 10 = 31
d	▲		▲ + 5
e	♥	Increase by 8	
f	◀	Increase by 17	
g		Decrease by 4	16 − 4 = 12
h		Decrease by 20	☐ − 20
i	▶	Decrease by 36	
j	✳		✳ − 9
k		Double	2 × ▇
l	✖	Double	
m	▼	Treble	

10 Each letter stands for a number. What is each number?

a $a + 1 = 7$	**b** $b - 2 = 12$	**c** $c \times 3 = 21$	**d** $5 + d = 14$
e $8 - e = 3$	**f** $4 \times f = 32$	**g** $g \div 3 = 11$	**h** $h \div 10 = 8$
i $23 - i = 3$	**j** $1 + j = 21$	**k** $k + k = 54$	**l** $l + l + l = 75$

11 $m = 12$ and $n = 8$. Find the value of these expressions.

a $m + 3$	**b** $n - 6$	**c** $4 \times m$	**d** $6 + n$
e $30 - m$	**f** $24 \div n$	**g** $m \div 3$	**h** $m \times n$

12 Copy and complete the table.

Start number	Change	Result
n	Increase by 5	$n + 5$
k	Increase by 47	
p	Decrease by 12	
q	Decrease by 20	
w	Double	
r		$r + 6$
t	Halve	
m		$m + n$

> explanation 3a   explanation 3b   explanation 3c

13 Write down the next two terms of each sequence. State whether the sequence is increasing or decreasing.

a 12, 14, 16, 18, ...	**b** 27, 24, 21, 18, ...	**c** 812, 712, 612, 512, ...
d 24, 40, 56, 72, ...	**e** 318, 338, 358, 378, ...	**f** 79, 68, 57, 46, ...
g 4, 8, 12, 16, ...	**h** 4, 8, 16, 32, ...	**i** 1, 10, 100, 1000, ...
*j 256, 128, 64, 32, ...	***k** 243, 81, 27, 9, ...	***l** 1, 1, 2, 3, 5, ...

14 Copy and complete these sequences.

a   1, 6, 11, ☐, 21, ☐

b   4, 7, ☐, 13, 16, ☐

c   2, ☐, 8, ☐, 14, 17, ☐

d   8, ☐, 18, ☐, 28, ☐

e   40, 31, ☐, 13, ☐

f   52, ☐, 44, ☐, 36, ☐

*g   2.5, 3, ☐, 4, ☐, ☐

*h   10, ☐, 9, ☐, 8, 7.5, ☐

*i   16, ☐, 19, ☐, ☐, 23.5

15 Copy and complete the table.

	Term	Term-to-term rule	First five terms
a	1st: 10	Add 4	
b	1st: 7	Double and then take away 5	
c	2nd: 21	Subtract 0.5	
d	2nd: 4	Divide by 2	
e	2nd: 13	Multiply by 3 and then add 1	
f	6th:		4, 9, 19, 39, 79
g	7th:		2.5, 5, 7.5, 10, 12.5

16 Most babies grow taller 2.5 cm each month in their first six months. Ben's height was 53 cm at birth.

a   Write a sequence that shows Ben's height each month until he is 6 months old.

b   Would you expect the sequence to continue in the same way? Explain your answer.

17 Here is a partly completed train timetable. Assume each journey takes the same time. Copy the timetable and fill in the missing times.

Exeter Central	14:14	15:33				
Pinhoe	14:19					
Whimple	14:26		16:26			
Feniton	14:31					
Honiton	14:37			17:07		
Axminster	14:48				18:18	

18 Halley's Comet last appeared in 1986. The years of its previous appearances make a sequence. The difference between consecutive terms isn't fixed. It varies between 75 and 79 years.

  a Copy and complete the table.

	79	77	79	77	78	75	76
Year							1531

	75	76	77	75	76	75	
Year				1910	1986		

  b When will the comet next appear?

explanation 4

19 The number of dots in the pattern makes a sequence.

Pattern			
Position	1	2	3
Term	3	6	9

Copy and complete.

4th term = 3 × ☐ = ☐   10th term = 3 × ☐ = ☐

50th term = ☐ × ☐ = ☐ nth term = ☐ × ☐

20 These are the position-to-term rules of some sequences. Write the first four terms of each sequence.

  a $n + 5$ **b** $n + 10$ **c** $n + 100$ **d** $n - 1$

  e $2 \times n$ **f** $5 \times n$ **g** $10 \times n$ **h** $11 \times n$

  i $n + 0.5$ **j** $n + 2.5$ **k** $n - 0.5$ **l** $n + 9.5$

21 Copy and complete the tables.

Even numbers	Position	1	2	3	n
	Term				

Odd numbers	Position	1	2	3	n
	Term				

Functions

- Using operations to make functions
- Applying an operation and its inverse
- How to use algebra to describe rules
- How to use a mapping diagram

Keywords

You should know

explanation 1

1 Here is a function machine.

input → | × 5 | → output

a Write the output for each of these input values.

   i 3   **ii** 11   **iii** 7   **iv** 21

b Write the input for each of these output values.

   i 20   **ii** 30   **iii** 35   **iv** 120

2 Copy and complete these function machines.

a 4, 7, □ → | + □ | → 15, □, 27

b 5, 8, 10 → | × □ | → □, 48, □

c 7, 14, 21 → | ÷ □ | → □, □, 3

d 10, □, n → | □ | → □, 22, $n - 8$

explanation 2

3 Draw a function machine for $x \to x + 10$ using the input values 0, 2, 11 and 17.

4 Draw a function machine for $x \to 3x$ using the input values 0, 0.5, 2 and 2.5.

5 Draw a function machine for $x \to 10x$ with output values 0, 10, 30 and 45.

6 Input and output values for some functions are shown below.

Write the rule for each function in the form $x \rightarrow \Box$

   a $1 \rightarrow 101$ **b** $21 \rightarrow 15$ **c** $2 \rightarrow 22$ **d** $12 \rightarrow 3$

         $2 \rightarrow 102$ $27 \rightarrow 21$ $4 \rightarrow 44$ $16 \rightarrow 4$

         $3 \rightarrow 103$ $30 \rightarrow 24$ $5 \rightarrow 55$ $20 \rightarrow 5$

---

explanation 3

7 Copy and complete these function machines.

   a 5   **b** 4

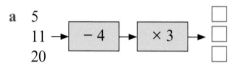
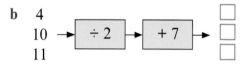

   c 3   **d** 4

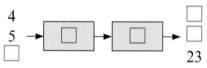

8 Copy and complete this function machine to show $x \rightarrow 2x + 7$.

9 Copy and complete this function machine to show $x \rightarrow \frac{x}{3} + 5$.

10 Copy and complete this function machine to show $x \rightarrow \frac{2x}{5}$.

11 Copy and complete this function machine to show $x \rightarrow 4 + 3x$.

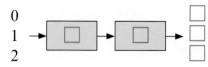

12 Information about some functions is shown below.

Copy and complete.

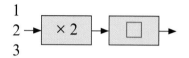

a $10 \rightarrow 2$
$12 \rightarrow 3$
$18 \rightarrow \square$
$x \rightarrow \dfrac{x}{2} - \square$

b $27 \rightarrow 12$
$36 \rightarrow 16$
$99 \rightarrow \square$
$x \rightarrow \dfrac{4x}{\square}$

c $5 \rightarrow 5$
$8 \rightarrow 14$
$\square \rightarrow 26$
$x \rightarrow 3x - \square$

d $0 \rightarrow \square$
$2 \rightarrow 23$
$\square \rightarrow 87$
$x \rightarrow \square\, x + 7$

13 Copy and complete the function machine to give these outputs:

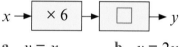

$\begin{array}{l} 1 \\ 2 \rightarrow \boxed{\times 2} \rightarrow \boxed{\ \square\ } \rightarrow \\ 3 \end{array}$

a $\begin{array}{l}1\\2\\3\end{array}$
b $\begin{array}{l}2\\4\\6\end{array}$
c $\begin{array}{l}10\\20\\30\end{array}$

14 Copy and complete the function machine for each value of y.

$x \rightarrow \boxed{\times 6} \rightarrow \boxed{\ \square\ } \rightarrow y$

a $y = x$ **b** $y = 2x$ **c** $y = 3x$ **d** $y = \dfrac{x}{2}$

explanation 4

15 Work out the missing operations for these function machines, which have the same input and output.

a $x \rightarrow \boxed{+5} \rightarrow \boxed{\ \ } \rightarrow x$ **b** $x \rightarrow \boxed{\ \ } \rightarrow \boxed{\div 9} \rightarrow x$

c $x \rightarrow \boxed{\ \ } \rightarrow \boxed{-7.2} \rightarrow x$ **d** $x \rightarrow \boxed{\times 99} \rightarrow \boxed{\ \ } \rightarrow x$

e $x \rightarrow \boxed{+8} \rightarrow \boxed{+6} \rightarrow \boxed{\ \ } \rightarrow x$

f $x \rightarrow \boxed{+9} \rightarrow \boxed{-5} \rightarrow \boxed{\ \ } \rightarrow x$

g $x \rightarrow \boxed{\ \ } \rightarrow \boxed{-5} \rightarrow \boxed{+20} \rightarrow x$

h $x \rightarrow \boxed{\times 3} \rightarrow \boxed{\ \ } \rightarrow \boxed{\div 12} \rightarrow x$

i $x \rightarrow \boxed{\times 5} \rightarrow \boxed{\times 4} \rightarrow \boxed{\ \ } \rightarrow x$

j $x \rightarrow \boxed{\times 3} \rightarrow \boxed{+2} \rightarrow \boxed{-2} \rightarrow \boxed{\ \ } \rightarrow x$

k $x \rightarrow \boxed{-7} \rightarrow \boxed{\div 5} \rightarrow \boxed{\ \ } \rightarrow \boxed{\ \ } \rightarrow x$

16 Write a simpler version of each function machine, replacing the two operations with one operation.

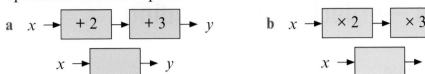

a $x \rightarrow \boxed{+2} \rightarrow \boxed{+3} \rightarrow y$

$x \rightarrow \boxed{} \rightarrow y$

b $x \rightarrow \boxed{\times 2} \rightarrow \boxed{\times 3} \rightarrow y$

$x \rightarrow \boxed{} \rightarrow y$

17 $10 \rightarrow \boxed{} \rightarrow \boxed{} \rightarrow \boxed{} \rightarrow \square$

Use the operations $\times 5$, -4 and $+7$ in the function machine.

a Make the largest output.

b Make the smallest output.

explanation 5

18 a Copy and complete the table of x and y values for this function machine.

$x \rightarrow \boxed{\times 2} \rightarrow \boxed{-6} \rightarrow y$

x	3	4	5	6	7	8	9	10	11	12	13
y											

b Copy and complete this mapping diagram using the values from your table.

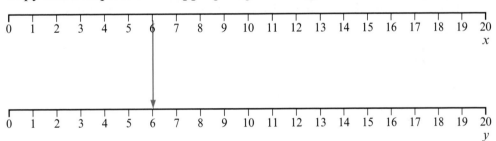

19 The function with rule $n \rightarrow 3n - 1$ uses the sequence 1, 2, 3, ... as input values.

The output values make a new sequence.

a Write down the first 10 terms of this new sequence.

b Does the number 239 belong to the new sequence? Explain how you know.

c How many terms of the new sequence are smaller than 50?

Decimals — ordering and rounding

- Reading decimals on a number line
- Comparing decimals
- Multipling and dividing decimals by 10, 100 and 1000
- Rounding whole numbers and decimals

Keywords

You should know

explanation 1a   explanation 1b

1 Write the value of each underlined digit as a fraction.

    a 2.7<u>6</u>5   **b** 0.91<u>4</u>   **c** 12.3<u>8</u>   **d** 36.9<u>5</u>

2 Write the value of each underlined digit in words.

    a 7.2<u>1</u>   **b** 0.2<u>8</u>7   **c** 124.3<u>8</u>   **d** 0.00<u>4</u>

3 Write these numbers in words.

    a $\dfrac{3}{10}$ **b** $\dfrac{7}{100}$ **c** $\dfrac{41}{1000}$ **d** $\dfrac{38}{100}$

4 Write these numbers as decimals.

    a Four and seven hundredths

    b Twelve and three tenths

    c Sixteen and five thousandths

    d Thirty-two and twenty-seven thousandths

5 Write each of these as a decimal number.

    a $5 + \dfrac{3}{10}$ **b** $23 + \dfrac{9}{100}$ **c** $2 + \dfrac{8}{10} + \dfrac{2}{100}$

    d $1 + \dfrac{3}{10} + \dfrac{8}{1000}$ **e** $9 + \dfrac{25}{100}$ **f** $1 + \dfrac{73}{1000}$

    g $34 + \dfrac{683}{1000}$ **h** $1 + \dfrac{1}{1000}$ **i** $3 + \dfrac{1}{100} + \dfrac{3}{1000}$

6 Here are some number lines. Write down the value at each of the labelled points.

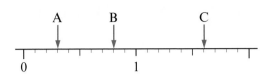 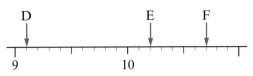

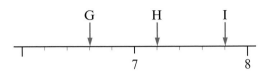 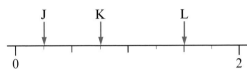

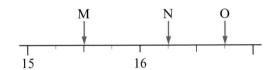 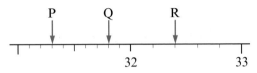

7 Here are some number lines. Write down the value at each of the labelled points.

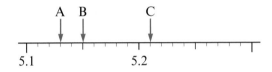 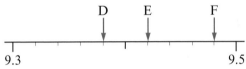

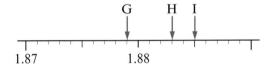 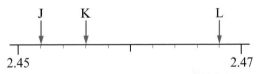

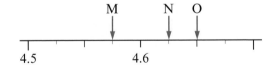 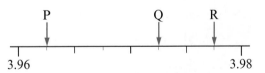

8 Find the decimal that is halfway between the numbers in each pair.

  a 3.6, 3.7   **b** 2.1, 2.2   **c** 3.9, 4   **d** 0, 0.1

  e 7.6, 8   **f** 5.36, 5.37   **g** 8.98, 9   **h** 0, 0.01

explanation 2

9 Work out these calculations.

  a 2.71×10 **b** $3.6 \div 10$ **c** 0.209×10 **d** 0.045×10

  e $0.37 \div 10$ **f** 2.8×10 **g** $37 \div 10$ **h** $673 \div 10$

10 Work out these calculations.

    a 1.2×100 **b** 3.42×100 **c** $67 \div 100$ **d** 100×0.57

    e $3.28 \div 100$ **f** $0.27 \div 100$ **g** 0.0286×100 **h** $239 \div 100$

11 Work out these calculations.

    a 0.18×1000 **b** $8 \div 1000$ **c** $2.01 \div 1000$ **d** 0.025×1000

    e $0.76 \div 1000$ **f** $400 \div 1000$ **g** $6781 \div 1000$ **h** 1000×0.006

12 A car on a motorway travels 27.8 m every second. Work out how far it travels in:

    a 10 seconds   **b** 1 minute 40 seconds

13 Diesel costs 99.7 p per litre. A truck driver pays for 1000 litres.

    a What is the cost in pence?   **b** What is the cost in pounds?

14 A pack of 100 biros weighs 950 g. How much does each biro weigh?

15 Bob is fitting a new kitchen. He wants all of the measurements to be in millimetres.

    Write each of the labelled measurements in millimetres.

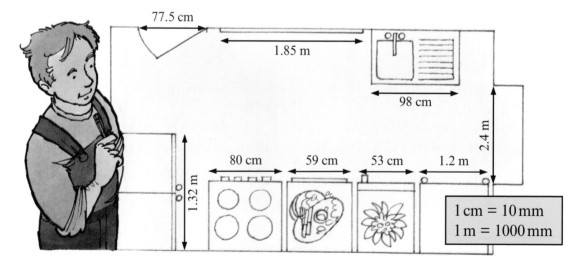

16 Find the value of the missing numbers.

   a $\square \times 0.003 = 0.03$ **b** $2.7 \div \square = 0.0027$ **c** $100 \times \square = 45$

   d $\square \div 1000 = 0.653$ **e** $10 \times \square = 0.09$ **f** $\square \div 10 = 8.6$

   g $4.2 \times \square = 4200$ **h** $\square \div 100 = 1.6$ **i** $0.281 \div \square = 0.0281$

17 Copy and complete these conversions.

   a $37.5\,\text{cm} = \square\,\text{mm}$ **b** $495\,\text{mm} = \square\,\text{cm}$ **c** $786\,\text{mm} = \square\,\text{m}$

   d $127\,\text{cm} = \square\,\text{m}$ **e** $1230\,\text{mm} = \square\,\text{m}$ **f** $3.2\,\text{m} = \square\,\text{mm}$

18 Convert these volumes.

> 1 litre = 1000 ml
> 1 litre = 100 cl

   a 3 litres to centilitres   **b** 270 cl to litres

   c 700 ml to centilitres   **d** 1200 ml to litres

   e 320 cl to millilitres   **f** 0.85 litres to centilitres

19 A standard wine bottle has a capacity of 75 cl. A magnum contains 1.5 litres and a jeroboam contains 3000 ml.

   a How many standard bottles are equivalent to a magnum?

   b How many standard bottles are equivalent to a jeroboam?

(explanation 3)

20 Write these numbers in order of size, starting with the smallest.

   a 6, 5.9, 5.849, 5.85, 5.4999   **b** 11.3, 11.56, 11.18, 11.29, 11.06

   c 0.278, 0.25, 0.3, 0.249, 0.28   **d** 7.127, 7.123, 7.12, 7.129, 7.192

   e 0.0738, 0.0729, 0.073, 0.0732   **f** 19.1, 19.09, 19.18, 19.099, 19.178

21 Write down the smallest of each of these sets of numbers as a decimal.

   a $\dfrac{7}{10}, \dfrac{19}{100}, 0.24, \dfrac{38}{100}, 0.275$ **b** $\dfrac{3}{10} + \dfrac{7}{100}, 0.41, \dfrac{3}{10} + \dfrac{9}{1000}, 0.39$

   c $\dfrac{9}{100} + \dfrac{8}{1000}, 0.092, 0.1, 0.099$ **d** $\dfrac{27}{100}, \dfrac{138}{1000}, \dfrac{3}{10}, 0.14, 0.139$

22 Copy and complete. Use < or >.

The first one has been done for you.

a   2.79 < 2.8

b   0.18 ☐ 0.179

c   2.409 ☐ 2.413

d   12.23 ☐ 12.229

e   32.001 ☐ 32.01

f   26.047 ☐ 26.0467

g $\dfrac{37}{100}$ ☐ $\dfrac{268}{1000}$

h $\dfrac{27}{100}$ ☐ $\dfrac{89}{1000}$

i $\dfrac{1}{10}$ ☐ $\dfrac{99}{1000}$

23 Match the following numbers to the labelled points on the number line.

2.798, 2.801, 2.778, 2.794, 2.816, 2.784

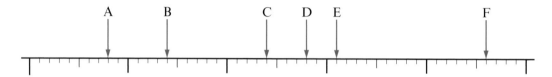

24 Copy and complete. Use < or >.

a   27 mm ☐ 2.5 cm

b   9.8 cm ☐ 9.7 m

c   240 cm ☐ 0.25 m

d   0.8 m ☐ 760 mm

e   58.2 cm ☐ 590 mm

f   3020 mm ☐ 3.1 m

25 Here are two digit cards separated by a decimal point.

Use any two of the digits from 9, 8, 7 and 2 to make a number. You can only use each digit once in any number that you make.

Make a list of all the possible numbers in order of size, largest first.

26 Each of the following clues refers to a number shown by an arrow on the number line below. Find the value of each letter.

a $a > 5.03$

b $b > 5$ and $b < 5.005$

c $c < 5$

d $5.01 < d < 5.02$

e $5.002 < e < 5.015$

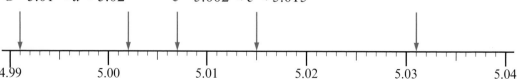

27 Copy the diagram.

Join the four smallest values in order.
Make a closed shape by joining to the
smallest value again.

If you are right, the diagram should let
you know! Explain.

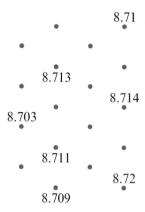

---

explanation 4

28 a Use the diagram to help you round each of these numbers to the nearest 10.

i 1623		**ii** 1639		**iii** 1644		**iv** 1602	
v 1654		**vi** 1605		**vii** 1597		**viii** 1635	

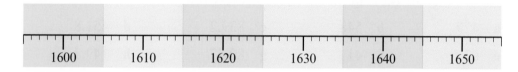

b Write the numbers where each of the yellow and
blue regions meet.

> ≤ means 'is
> less than or
> equal to'.

c The number x is 1620 to the nearest 10. What colour is
the region containing x?

d Copy and complete. $\square \leq x < \square$

e The number y is 1650 to the nearest 10. Copy and complete. $\square \leq y < \square$

29 a Use the diagram to help you round each of these numbers to the nearest 10.

i 1014		**ii** 986		**iii** 975		**iv** 992	
v 998		**vi** 1005		**vii** 1024		**viii** 969	

b The number x is 1010 to the nearest 10. Copy and complete. $\square \leq x < \square$

c The number y is 980 to the nearest 10. Copy and complete. $\square \leq y < \square$

30 Strawberry pickers are paid at the end of each day. Sam likes to keep his accounts simple, so he pays everyone to the nearest £10 on what they earn.

   a Work out how much Sam pays to each picker.

      i Rob earns £37   **ii** Tara earns £63

     iii Phil earns £54   **iv** Ravi earns £78

      v Fran earns £74.50   **vi** Kate earns £65

     vii Jack earns £57.41   **viii** Salma earns £82.29

      ix Tim earns £59.78

   b How much more did Fran need to earn to be paid an extra £10?

   c Sam pays James £60.

      i What is the least amount that James might have earned?

     ii What is the greatest amount that James might have earned?

31 Round each of these numbers to the nearest 100.

   a 479   **b** 548   **c** 839.2   **d** 451.8

   e 67.5   **f** 41   **g** 80.27   **h** 149.3

   i 1783   **j** 4709   **k** 21 386   **l** 17 449

32 Here are the attendance figures for the first game in a football season. Round each to the nearest thousand.

   a Real Madrid 64 867   **b** Le Mans 32 131   **c** Hamburg 49 713

   d Millwall 10 012   **e** Luton Town 8131   **e** Stoke City 8971

explanation 5

33 Use the diagram to help you round these decimals to the nearest whole number.

a   9.4   b   7.7   c   5.5   d   7.48

e   9.75   f   8.51   g   10.47   h   6.6002

34 Use the diagram to help you round these decimals to one decimal place.

a   8.93   b   8.66   c   9.04   d   8.74

e   8.75   f   9.048   g   8.863   h   9.119

35 Round each of these amounts to the nearest pound.

a   £8.47   b   £3.52   c   £12.70   d   £19.73

e   £37.56   f   £11.11   g   £96.45   h   £87.50

36 a What is the least amount that would round to £20 to the nearest pound?

b What is the greatest amount that would round to £20 to the nearest pound?

c What is the least amount that would round to £20 to the nearest £10?

d What is the greatest amount that would round to £20 to the nearest £10?

37 Fred is baffled. He is trying to place a stack of 10 boxes into the back of his van.

He knows that each box is 15 cm high, to the nearest centimetre. He also knows that the gap between the floor and the roof of his van is 1.5 m to the nearest 0.1 m.

The problem is that the boxes won't fit!

Explain why this might be.

Negative numbers

- Using a number line for positive and negative numbers
- Adding and subtracting negative numbers

Keywords

You should know

explanation 1

Decreasing   Increasing

–10 –9 –8 –7 –6 –5 –4 –3 –2 –1   0   1   2   3   4   5   6   7   8   9   10

1 Use the number line to help you find the missing terms in these sequences.

a 4, 2, 0, ☐, ☐, ☐   b 5, 3, 1, ☐, ☐, ☐   c 6, 3, 0, ☐, ☐, ☐

d −3, −1, 1, ☐, ☐, ☐   e −4, −2, 0, ☐, ☐, ☐   f 8, 5, ☐, ☐, −4, ☐

g 10, ☐, 4, ☐, −2, ☐   h −9, ☐, −1, ☐, 7, ☐   i −5, ☐, 0, ☐, ☐, 7.5

2 Describe each of the sequences in question **1** as either increasing or decreasing.

3 Write these numbers in order of size, smallest first.

a 4, 7, −3, 0, −2, −5   b 6, −4, −10, 3, −5, 0

c 0, 2, −1, −9, −3, −6   d 2.3, −1, −3, −4.2, −3.8

e −1.2, −0.7, 0.1, 7.2, −2   f 1, −7.2, −1.8, −3, −1.75

4 Copy and complete. Use the symbols < and >
to compare these pairs of numbers.

| < means 'is less than' |
| > means 'is greater than' |

a −6 ☐ −3   b 0 ☐ −2   c −7 ☐ −10   d −1 ☐ 8

e −31 ☐ −20   f −15 ☐ −19   g −5.2 ☐ −5   h −4.9 ☐ −5

5 Increase each of these numbers by 5.

a 7   b −2   c −8   d −5

e −9   f −1   g −20   h −100

6 Decrease each of these numbers by 7.

   a 11   **b** 3   **c** 0   **d** 2

   e −1   **f** −4   **g** −30   **h** −50

7 One morning in March, the outside temperature was −3°C. By midday this had risen to 12°C. By how much had the temperature increased?

8 On a cold day, wind chill can make it *feel* even colder. If the wind chill is −10°C, then a temperature of 4°C would feel like −6°C. What does each of these temperatures feel like with a wind chill of −10°C?

   a 1°C   **b** 3°C   **c** −2°C   **d** −15°C

explanation 2

9 Write down the calculation represented by each diagram.

   a 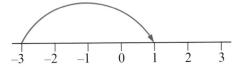   **b**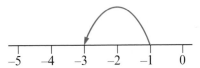

   c 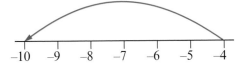   **d**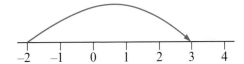

10 Work out the calculations, using the number line.

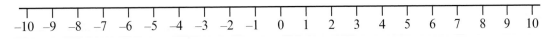

   a 3 − 8   **b** −9 + 7   **c** −3 − 6   **d** −8 + 1

   e −10 + 10   **f** −5 + 15   **g** −3 + 11   **h** −6 + 12

11 Work out the following calculations.

   a −7 + 3 + 1   **b** −9 + 5 + 7   **c** 2 − 6 − 4   **d** −10 + 5 + 9

12 Add 6 to each of the numbers, using the number line.

   a 2.5   **b** −0.5   **c** −3.5   **d** −7.5

13 Subtract 4 from each of these numbers.

a 3.5   b 1.5   c −2.5   d −5.5

14 Add 7.5 to each of these numbers.

a −3   b −1   c −8   d −10

e −2.5   f −5.5   g −7.5   h −9.5

15 Use the number line to help you find these values.

a −2 is decreased by 0.4   b −3 is increased by 0.2

c −1 is decreased by 0.9   d 0.3 is added to −1

e 1.1 is subtracted from −2   f 2 is added to −0.4

16 Copy and complete these calculations.

a −6 + ☐ = 3   b 2 − ☐ = −8   c −1 + ☐ = 6   d −3 ☐☐ = −7

e −5 ☐☐ = 3   f −7 ☐☐ = −10   g −2 ☐☐ = −6   h −4 ☐☐ = 1

i ☐ + 8 = 7   j ☐ − 6 = −4   k ☐ + 5 = −4   l ☐ − 9 = −10

explanation 3

17 Copy and complete the table to show two sets of equivalent instructions.

Instruction using positive numbers	Instruction using negative numbers
Move 3 places to the left	
	Move −5 places up
	Increase by −3
	Move −8 places to the right
Decrease by 4	

18 The diagram shows the path taken by a robot. The first two stages can be described as right 1, up −1.
Describe the remaining stages in the same way, without using left or down.

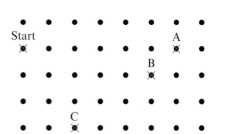

19 a Copy the diagram and draw the path described by these instructions.
right 3, up 1, right 1, up −3, right 2, up 1, right 1, up −2, right −4, up 2, right −1, up −2

b Which of the points A, B or C is the finish point?

20 Rewrite the following statements without using negative numbers.

a The ship travelled −50 miles north.

b In the evening, the temperature rose by −8 °C.

c As the plane approached the airport, it gained −5000 ft in height.

d The car that Peter bought last year is now worth −£3200 more.

e The population of the UK has fallen by −10 million since 1950.

explanation 4a   explanation 4b

21 Copy and complete the following statements.

a Adding −4 is the same as ...

b Subtracting −10 is the same as ...

c $1 + -4 = 1 \square 4 = \square$

d $16 - -10 = 16 \square 10 = \square$

e ... is the same as adding 9.

f ... is the same as subtracting 5.

g $-3 - \square = -3 + 9 = \square$

h $2 + \square = 2 - 5 = \square$

22 Work out these calculations.

a $-2 + -6$ **b** $4 - -5$ **c** $-3 - -3$ **d** $-4 - -7$

e $8 + -9$ **f** $0 - -4$ **g** $-10 + -1$ **h** $-12 - -13$

i $-3 - -2$ **j** $5 + -6$ **k** $10 + -0.5$ **l** $3.5 - -0.5$

23 Copy and complete these calculations.

a $-5 - -7 = -5 \,\square\, 7 = \square$

b $3 + -10 = 3 \,\square\, 10 = \square$

c $-8 \,\square\, -9 = -8 \,\square\, 9 = 1$

d $5 + \square = 5 - \square = -6$

e $-4 \,\square\, -3 = -4 \,\square\, 3 = -7$

f $\square + -8 = -10$

g $\square - -9 = -1$

h $-6 + \square = -11$

24 Copy and complete these addition and subtraction grids.

a

+	−7	3	0	
	−11			
−2				−6
0				
		−2		

−	−1	−3		6
5	6			
−3			−8	
		0		
−7				

c

−	2	4	−6	
−3	−5			
2				
	−3			
−5			−4	

+	1	−4	−1	
	−3			−7
−5				
−2				
				−9

25 In a magic square, each row, column and diagonal has the same total. Copy and complete these two magic squares.

a

2	0	−7	9
	5		−2
	−6		
−3		6	

b

7			−6
		−1	4
−2	3		
0		6	−5

26 Copy and complete these addition pyramids.

a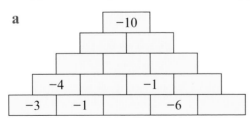

b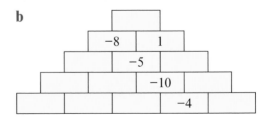

27 a Find two numbers that have a sum of 4 and a difference of 10.

b Find three consecutive numbers that total −12.

c If $20 + x < 20$, what can you say about x?

Multiples, factors and primes

- Finding multiples of a number
- Finding all of the factors of a number
- Using the relationship between multiples and factors
- Recognising prime numbers and prime factors

Keywords

You should know

explanation 1

1 The red dots on the diagram show the first six multiples of 3.

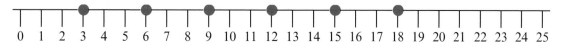

   a What is the difference between any multiple of 3 and the next multiple of 3?

   b What are the next two multiples of 3 after 18?

   c What is the tenth multiple of 3?

   d What is the hundredth multiple of 3?

2 The multiples of 5 make a sequence. Write down:

   a the first six terms   **b** the tenth term   **c** the twentieth term

   d the number of terms less than 60   **e** the largest term less than 200.

3 The multiples of 17 make a sequence. One term in the sequence is 323.

   a What is the next term in the sequence?

   b What is the previous term?

4 John thinks of a whole number that is greater than 1. The red dots below show multiples of John's number.

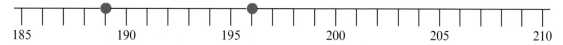

   a What is John's number?

   b Write down the next two multiples of this number after 196.

5 The square contains all the numbers from 1 to 49. Some of the numbers are hidden.

43	●	25	1	●	11	7
35	29	37	●	20	15	49
5	22	21	12	41	38	9
39	45	2	6	27	33	13
●	30	18	26	36	4	31
44	28	42	34	3	47	17
●	14	46	19	10	●	23

   a Describe the numbers highlighted in yellow.

   b How many multiples of 9 are shown?

   c What is the largest multiple of 11 shown?

   d The hidden numbers are multiples of the same number. What are the hidden numbers?

6 How many multiples of 3 would be shown on a 100 square?

> explanation 2a   explanation 2b

7 Find the lowest common multiple of each set of numbers.

a 5, 3	**b** 8, 6	**c** 10, 5	**d** 4, 7
e 3, 9	**f** 12, 24	**g** 7, 8	**h** 20, 30
i 2, 4, 8	**j** 5, 10, 15	**k** 6, 8, 12	**l** 3, 4, 5

8 Describe each statement as true or false.

   If the statement is false, give a counter-example.

   a Any multiple of 8 is also a multiple of 4.

   b Any multiple of 3 is also a multiple of 6.

   c A common multiple of 6 and 4 is 24.

   d You can always find a common multiple of a pair of numbers by multiplying them together.

   e Multiplying a pair of numbers never gives their lowest common multiple.

The winner's number is always a multiple of 5.

9 The number 12 is the lowest common multiple of two numbers. One of those numbers is also 12. What is the other number? Write down as many possibilities as you can.

10 The hot tap alone will fill a bath in 6 minutes. The cold tap alone will take
4 minutes.

a   Both taps are used together. Is the time needed to fill the bath more or less
than 4 minutes?

b   Find the lowest common multiple of 6 and 4.

c   Explain why your answer to part **b** gives
the time needed to fill the bath five times.

d   How long would it take to
fill the bath once?

(explanation 3)

11 Describe each of the following statements as true or false.
If the statement is true, write a multiplication that matches it.

The first one is done for you.

a   3 is a factor of 15   True, $3 \times 5 = 15$ b   8 is a factor of 32

c   9 is a factor of 27   d   6 is a factor of 14

e   11 is a factor of 32   f   16 is a factor of 48

g   25 is a factor of 100   h   12 is a factor of 72

i   7 is a factor of 45   j   21 is a factor of 105

12 Copy and complete the diagram to show the factor pairs of 12.

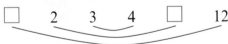

13 Draw a diagram to show the factor pairs of each number.

a   24   b   32   c   27   d   56

14 List all the factors of each number.

a   30   b   28   c   60   d   108

e   125   f   72   g   84   h   64

15 3384 is a multiple of 72, and 36 is a factor of 72. Write two statements that
connect 36 and 3384.

16 p and q represent whole numbers and p is a factor of q. Which of the statements *must* be true?

    a q is a factor of p **b** q is a multiple of p

    c p is a factor of $2 \times q$ **d** q is a factor of $10 \times p$

> explanation 4

17 Machine A takes two input numbers and gives their common factors as the output numbers.

Find the output for each input.

    a 8, 12   **b** 15, 30   **c** 18, 24

    d 24, 40   **e** 32, 128   **f** 27, 29

    g 36, 45   **h** 27, 81   **i** 84, 144

Machine A

18 Machine B takes any number of input numbers. The highest input number is given as the output number.

    a Put 36 and 45 into Machine A and then put the output values into Machine B. What is the output from Machine B?

    b What is the connection between your answer to part **b** and the numbers 36 and 45?

Machine B

19 Find the highest common factor of each set of numbers.

    a 12, 18   **b** 21, 42   **c** 33, 77   **d** 44, 88

    e 35, 49   **f** 4000, 4500   **g** 26, 78   **h** 260, 780

    i 8, 12, 24   **j** 30, 60, 75   **k** 44, 88, 121   **l** 36, 90, 180

20 a Write down two numbers. The smaller number must be the highest common factor of the pair of numbers.

    b What is the lowest common multiple of the pair of numbers?

> explanation 5

21 a Write down all the factors of each number.

      i 2   **ii** 1   **iii** 7   **iv** 22

    b Which of the numbers in part **a** are prime numbers?

22 a List all the prime numbers less than 20.

b How many even prime numbers are there?

23 a Find pairs of prime numbers that add together to make each of these numbers. Find as many pairs as you can.

i 12   **ii** 16   **iii** 24   **iv** 32

b Which of the numbers in part **a** can be written as the sum of two primes in only one way?

24 a Find a pair of prime numbers that multiply together to make each of these numbers.

i 21   **ii** 55   **iii** 26   **iv** 51   **v** 143   **vi** 38   **vii** 57   **viii** 95

b Is it possible to find a different answer for any of the numbers in part **a**?

25 List all the prime numbers between 20 and 50.

26 Twin primes are prime numbers that differ by 2.

The first pair of twin primes are 3 and 5.

Find the values of the next four twin primes.

(**explanation 6**) ───────────────────────────────────

27 a Which factors of 12 are prime numbers?

b Copy and complete using the prime factors of 12.

$12 = \square \times \square \times \square$

> You can use a factor more than once.

28 Copy and complete using the prime factors of each number.

a $10 = \square \times \square$

b $18 = \square \times \square \times \square$

c $8 = \square \times \square \times \square$

d $30 = \square \times \square \times \square$

e $36 = \square \times \square \times \square \times \square$

f $100 = \square \times \square \times \square \times \square$

29 Only one of the numbers below is prime. Which number is it and how do you know?

7870   7883   7864   7795

Patterns, squares and roots

- Calculating square numbers and square roots
- Recognising the relationship between odd numbers and square numbers
- Identifying triangular numbers
- Recognising the relationship between triangular numbers and square numbers

Keywords

You should know

explanation 1

1 Here is a sequence of diagrams showing the square numbers 1, 4 and 9.

$$1^2 = 1 \times 1$$
$$= 1$$

$$2^2 = 2 \times 2$$
$$= 4$$

$$3^2 = 3 \times 3$$
$$= 9$$

a Copy and continue the pattern to show the next two square numbers.

b Copy and complete the table.

You should learn the square numbers.

n	1	2	3	4	5	6	7	8	9	10	11	12	13	14	15
n^2															

2 Find the square number between each pair of numbers.

a 11, 17　　　**b** 23, 31　　　**c** 57, 66　　　**d** 70, 82

e 101, 130　　　**f** 200, 250　　　**g** 180, 200　　　**h** 59.8, 72.6

3 Work out these calculations.

a $7^2 + 1^2$　　　**b** $3^2 + 4^2$　　　**c** $4^2 + 8^2$　　　**d** $10^2 - 7^2$

e $6^2 - 5^2$　　　**f** Twice 3^2　　　**g** Half of 8^2　　　**h** $6^2 \div 4$

4 Copy and complete the following calculations.

a $3^2 + 4^2 = \square^2$　　　**b** $13^2 - 12^2 = \square^2$　　　**c** $10^2 - \square^2 = 6^2$

5 **a** Write two consecutive odd numbers. Multiply them together, and then add 1. Repeat the process several times with different numbers.

   b What do you notice about your final answers?

   c What happens if you start with even numbers instead?

6 **a** Copy and complete the diagram to show the factor pairs of 16.

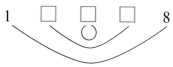

   b Draw a diagram to show the factor pairs of 36.

   c What can you say about the number of factors of a square number? Explain your answer.

> **explanation 2**

7 Write the value of each of these.

   a $\sqrt{16}$ **b** $\sqrt{100}$ **c** $\sqrt{36}$ **d** $\sqrt{144}$

   e $\sqrt{49}$ **f** $\sqrt{25}$ **g** $\sqrt{64}$ **h** $\sqrt{169}$

   i $\sqrt{121}$ **j** $\sqrt{225}$ **k** $\sqrt{1}$ **l** $\sqrt{0}$

   m $2 \times \sqrt{64}$ **n** $5 \times \sqrt{9}$ **o** $\sqrt{4} \times \sqrt{196}$ **p** $32 \div \sqrt{16}$

8 **a** Copy and complete: $\sqrt{900} = \sqrt{9} \times \sqrt{100} = \square \times \square = \square$

   b Use the method of part **a** to work out these square roots:

   i $\sqrt{400}$ **ii** $\sqrt{2500}$ **iii** $\sqrt{1600}$ **iv** $\sqrt{4900}$

9 $\sqrt{10}$ is not a whole number.

   You can tell that $\sqrt{10}$ lies between 3 and 4 because $3 \times 3 = 9$ and $4 \times 4 = 16$.

   Copy and complete the following statements by using two consecutive numbers.

   a $\sqrt{3}$ lies between $\square$ and $\square$ because ...

   b $\sqrt{20}$ lies between $\square$ and $\square$ because ...

10 These diagrams show square numbers. They show the relationship between square numbers and odd numbers.

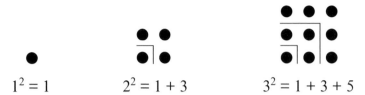

$1^2 = 1$ $2^2 = 1 + 3$ $3^2 = 1 + 3 + 5$

a Copy and continue the pattern for the next three square numbers.

b Copy and complete.

   i The sum of the first 5 odd numbers is $\square^2$.

   ii The sum of the first 10 odd numbers is $\square^2$.

c What is the sum of the first 100 odd numbers?

   Use what you know about square numbers to help you.

11 This diagram shows the first three triangular numbers.

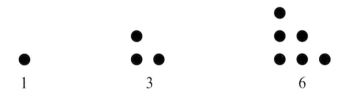

   1   3   6

a Copy and continue the pattern to show the first six triangular numbers.

b The first three square numbers are shown here. What connection do you think there is between triangular numbers and square numbers?

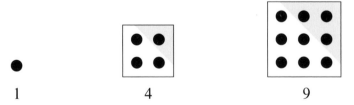

   1   4   9

c Find these sums.

   i The 9th and 10th triangular numbers

   ii The 99th and 100th triangular numbers

Adding and subtracting

- Adding and subtracting decimals
- Using addition and subtraction of decimals to solve problems

Keywords

You should know

explanation 1

1 Work out each sum.

a 16.3 + 7.25

b 0.146 + 2.59

c 5.23 + 11.9 + 6

d 2.31 + 17.5 + 1.47

e 32 + 4.76 + 12.38

f 0.076 + 0.14 + 2.83

2 Work out these amounts.

a £8.50 + £2.75

b £4.32 + £6.71

c £10 + £4.98

d £4.63 + £3.21 + £7.46

e £12.04 + £8.54 + 2.52

f £11.37 + 70p + £4.68

3 Copy and complete these calculations.

a
```
    2.■8
  +1■.37
  ─────
  ■2.8■
```

b
```
   17.■9
  +2■.3■
  ─────
  ■2.04
```

c
```
  ■8.■2
 +23.7■
 ─────
 4■.21
```

d
```
   48.■3
   1■.71
  +■2.8■
  ─────
  ■4.81
```

4 Copy and complete these addition pyramids.

a

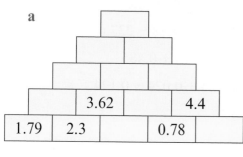

b

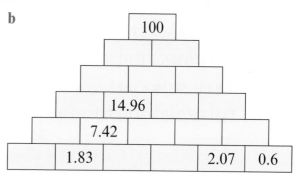

5 The diagram shows a magic star. The numbers lying on each line have the same total.

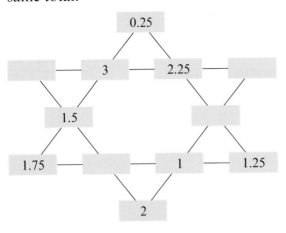

a Copy and complete the magic star using the numbers 2.5, 0.75, 2.75, 0.5.

*b This magic star has two more properties based on sums. Find them.

explanation 2

6 Work out each difference.

  a 39.4 − 8.7   **b** 9.45 − 1.637   **c** 76.8 − 9.651

  d 456 − 67.83   **e** 1.78 − 0.3486   **f** 234.68 − 97

7 **a** £58.20 − £7.14   **b** £13.26 − £8.42   **c** £27.50 − £11.25

   d £112.49 − £14.98   **e** £257.07 − £66.47   **f** £45.87 − 98p

8 Work these out. You will have to do two calculations for each.

  a 5.37 + 6.28 − 7.9   **b** 12.3 − 6.74 + 8.6

  c 82.6 − 19.8 − 7.53   **d** 500 − 123.78 − 237.6

  e 0.79 + 0.0286 − 0.0179   **f** 27 − 3.14 + 0.486

  g 145.82 − 54.28 − 0.12   **h** 0.725 + 0.024 − 0.124

  i 1.245 − 0.248 + 0.0178

9 Copy and complete these calculations.

a
```
   9 . 7 □ 3
 - 4 . □ 7 □
 ─────────────
   □ . 3 9 2
```

b
```
   □ 5 . □ 7
 - 2 7 . 1 □
 ─────────────
   3 □ . 8 9
```

c
```
   8 . 1 □ 0
 - □ . □ 3 □
 ─────────────
   3 . 1 5 4
```

d
```
   □ . 2 1 □
 - 3 . □ □ 6
 ─────────────
   1 . 8 5 3
```

e
```
   □ . 6 3 1
 - 1 . 4 □ 8
 ─────────────
   1 . □ 0 □
```

f
```
   3 . 4 1 □
 - □ . □ 0 6
 ─────────────
   1 . 9 □ 6
```

g
```
   4 . 8 □ 2
 - □ . 7 2 □
 ─────────────
   1 . □ 9 9
```

h
```
   □ . 3 5 □
 - 1 . □ 6 1
 ─────────────
   7 . 9 □ 7
```

10 The diagrams below show some scales with weights given in grams.

Find the value of the missing weights to make the scales balance.

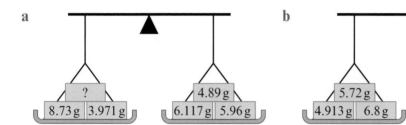

a
? / 4.89 g
8.73 g   3.971 g / 6.117 g   5.96 g

b
5.72 g / 7.25 g
4.913 g   6.8 g / ?   4.91 g

11 Four teams took part in the 4 × 100 m relay event on sports day.

The times for each leg of the race are shown in the table in seconds.

	Team			
Stage	**Red**	**Blue**	**Green**	**Yellow**
1st leg	14.71	15.03	15.13	14.98
2nd leg	13.92	14.79	14.64	15.16
3rd leg	15.1	14.48	14.42	14.05
4th leg	13.83	13.97	13.29	14.23

a Which team was leading at the end of the second leg?

b Which team won the race?

c What was the winning time?

d What was the difference between the times of the first two teams?

e What was the difference in times between the first and last teams?

Length and perimeter

- Measuring and drawing to the nearest millimetre
- Estimating distances using appropriate units
- Calculating the perimeter of a figure

Keywords

You should know

explanation 1

1 Measure the length of each line. Give your answers to the nearest 0.1 cm.

a _____

b _____

c _____

d _____

2 **a** Measure the length of each line. Give your answers to the nearest millimetre.

i   ii   iii

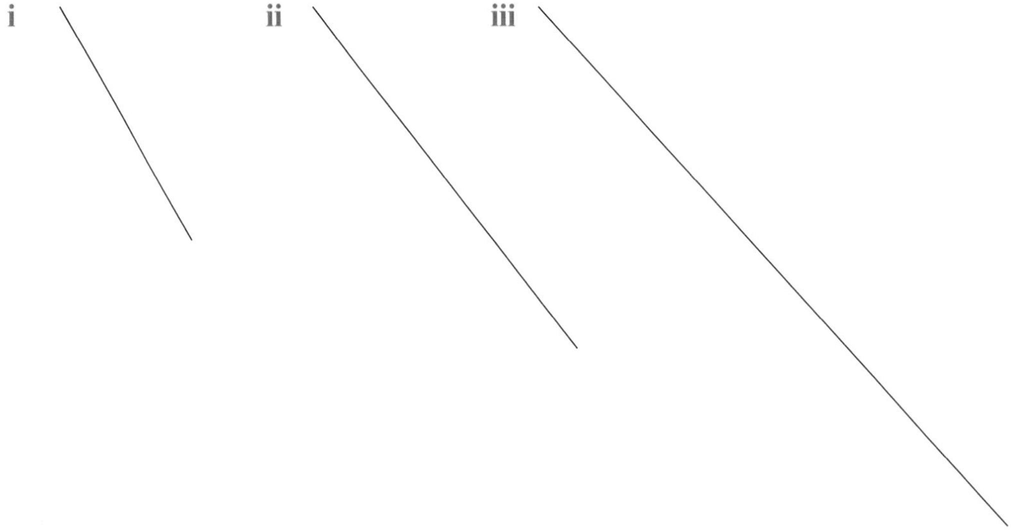

b One of the lines has the same length as a line in question **1**. Which lines are they?

3 **a** Draw each of the diagrams below as accurately as you can using the measurements shown.

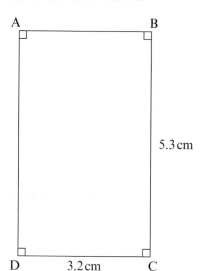

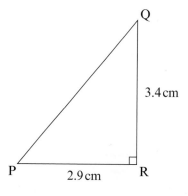

b Measure these distances to the nearest 0.1 cm.

    i AC   **ii** BD   **iii** PQ

c What do you notice about the lengths of AC and BD?

4 Here are two pictures of computer monitors. The screen size is measured along a diagonal of the rectangle containing the picture.

  a Measure each screen size as shown to the nearest 0.1 cm.

  b The real screen sizes are ten times the sizes shown here.

    Write down the real screen size in each case.

    i   **ii**

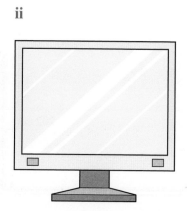

explanation 2

5 Choose from the numbers and units given in the table to make the measurements described below. Pictures are not drawn to scale.

Numbers	Units
105, 0.05, 5.4, 27, 68, 11	mm, cm, m

Wingspan of bumblebee

Height of giraffe

Choose the most sensible units first, then look for a suitable number.

Length of a tennis racquet

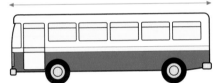

Length of a bus

Thickness of a human hair

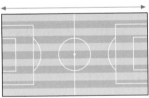

Length of Wembley pitch

6 The diagram shows the path to be followed by cable linking two telephone sockets. The cable passes over a doorway at a height of 202 cm.

How much cable is needed?

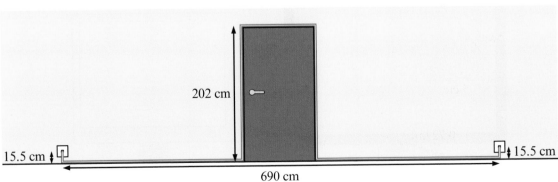

202 cm

15.5 cm

15.5 cm

690 cm

explanation 3

7 Work out the perimeter of each of these rectangles.

a

24 cm

41 cm

b   17 mm

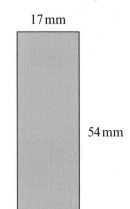

54 mm

c   14 m

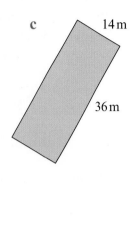

36 m

8 Work out the perimeter of each of these squares.

a

28 cm

b

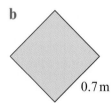

0.7 m

c

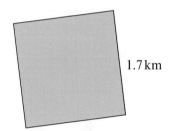

1.7 km

9 The perimeter of a square is 84 cm. What is the length of each side?

10 Work out the perimeter of each of these quadrilaterals.

a

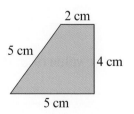
2 cm
5 cm
4 cm
5 cm

b

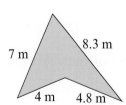
8.3 m
7 m
4 m   4.8 m

c

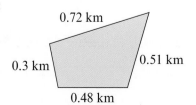
0.72 km
0.3 km
0.51 km
0.48 km

d

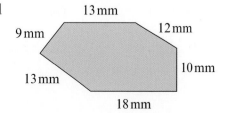
13 mm
9 mm
12 mm
13 mm
10 mm
18 mm

11   **a**   Work out the perimeter of the shape below.

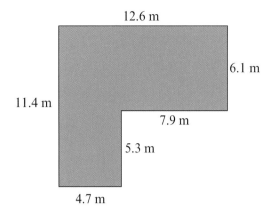

    b   Show that the perimeter can be worked out by adding two of the lengths
shown and doubling the answer.

12   Work out the perimeter of each of these figures.

a

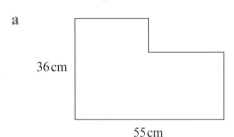

b

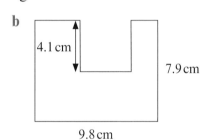

c

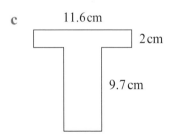

d

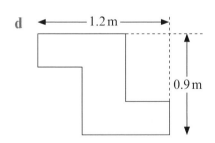

13   The perimeter of each of these figures is 30 m. Calculate the value of a, b and c.

a

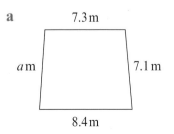

b

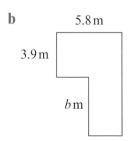

c

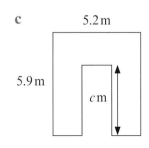

14 a Without working out the perimeters, find which of the shapes below have the same perimeter as this rectangle.

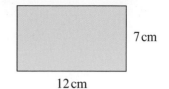

7 cm

12 cm

b Find the perimeter of each shape.

i
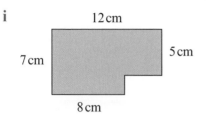

12 cm

5 cm

7 cm

8 cm

ii
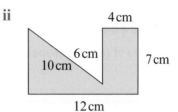

4 cm

6 cm

10 cm

7 cm

12 cm

iii
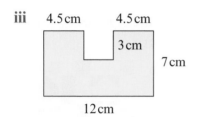

4.5 cm   4.5 cm

3 cm

7 cm

12 cm

iv
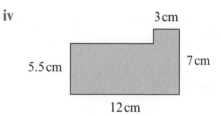

3 cm

5.5 cm

7 cm

12 cm

v
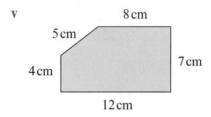

8 cm

5 cm

7 cm

4 cm

12 cm

vi
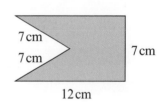

7 cm

7 cm

7 cm

12 cm

vii
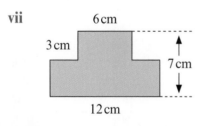

6 cm

3 cm

7 cm

12 cm

15 Find the perimeter of this shape.

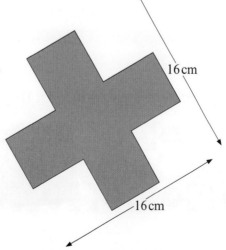

16 cm

16 cm

Area

- Finding the areas of shapes based on rectangles
- Converting between cm^2 and mm^2
- Finding the area of a triangle
- Estimating the area of complex shapes

Keywords

You should know

explanation 1

1 Here are some mosaic tile patterns. All of the tiles are squares of this size ■.
Work out the number of tiles needed for each pattern.

a
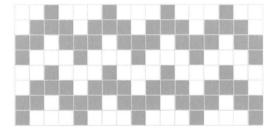

b
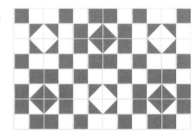

c
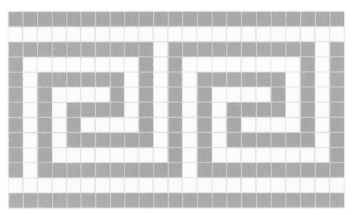

d

2 This mosaic pattern is partly hidden. How many square tiles does it contain?

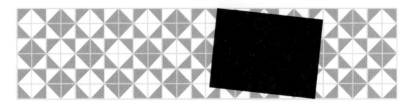

3 How many one centimetre square tiles would fit inside this rectangle?

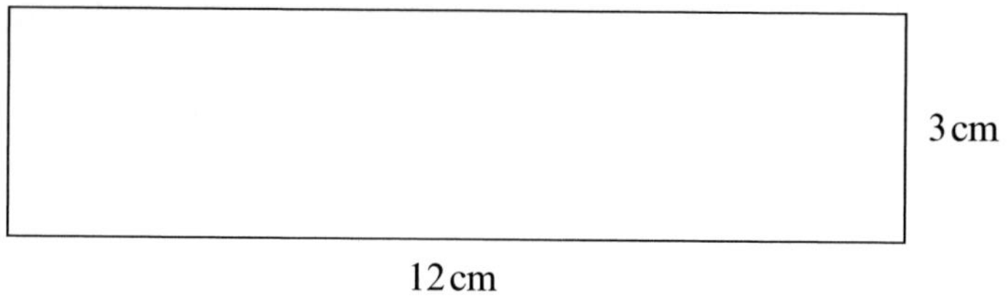

3 cm

12 cm

explanation 2

4 Work out the area of each of these rectangles.

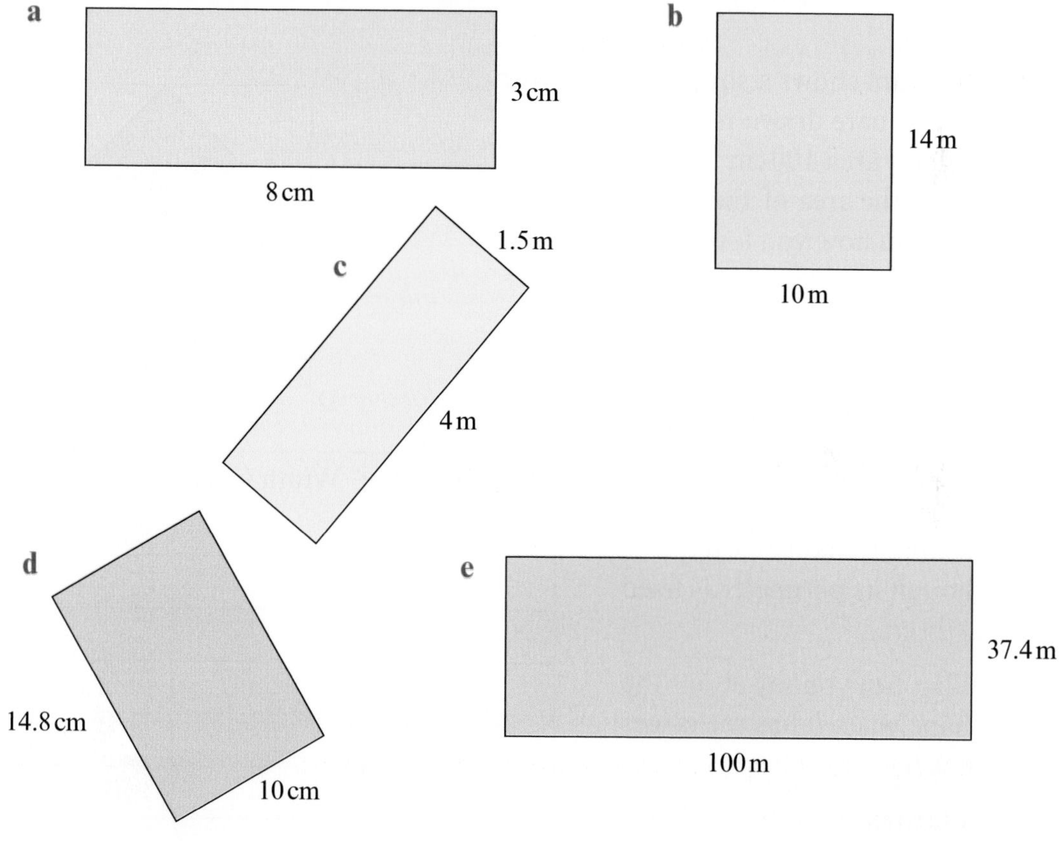

a

3 cm

8 cm

b

14 m

10 m

c

1.5 m

4 m

d

14.8 cm

10 cm

e

37.4 m

100 m

5 Find the area of this rectangle in square millimetres.

Remember
1 cm = 10 mm

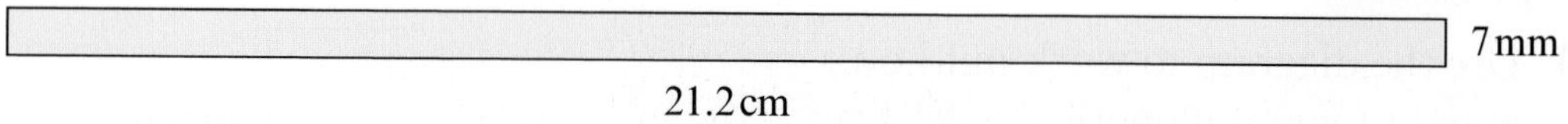

7 mm

21.2 cm

41

6 Find the area of each square.

a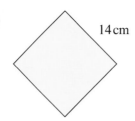

8 m

b

14 cm

c

17 mm

7 **a** Work out the area of a square with perimeter 36 cm.

b Work out the perimeter of a square with area 121 m².

8 The diagram shows a square ABCD with
a yellow square drawn inside.
ABCD has area 100 cm².
Calculate the area of the yellow square
and explain how you found your answer.

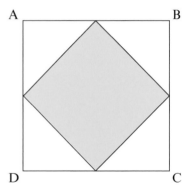

9 **a** Copy and complete the table
showing how the area of a
rectangle changes, even
though its perimeter is fixed
at 24 cm.

Length (cm)	Width (cm)	Area (cm²)
11	1	
10		
9		
8		
7		
6		

b What can you say about the
shape when it has the largest
area?

c A farmer has 80 m of fence
and wants to construct a
rectangular enclosure with
the largest possible area. What is this area?

*10 Use the diagram to work out how
many square millimetres make 1 cm².

10 mm

1 cm   10 mm

1 cm

explanation 3

11 Copy and complete these area calculations.

a

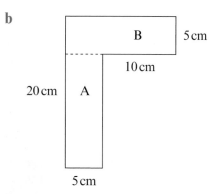

Area A = 5 cm × 20 cm = ☐
Area B = ☐ × ☐ = ☐
Total area = ☐

b

Area A = 5 cm × 15 cm = ☐
Area B = ☐ × ☐ = ☐
Total area = ☐

12 What does question **11** show about calculating the total area of a shape?

13 Work out the area of each of these shapes.

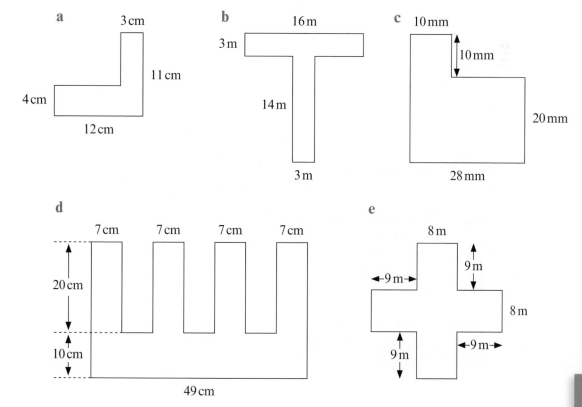

a
3 cm
11 cm
4 cm
12 cm

b
16 m
3 m
14 m
3 m

c
10 mm
10 mm
20 mm
28 mm

d
7 cm 7 cm 7 cm 7 cm
20 cm
10 cm
49 cm

e
8 m
9 m
←9 m→
8 m
9 m
←9 m→

explanation 4

14 This mosaic pattern
includes an area where
there are no tiles.
How many tiles are used
in the pattern?

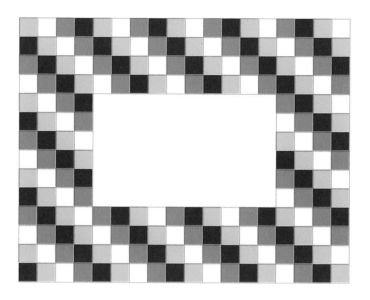

15 Work out the coloured areas of these diagrams.

a

3 m

11 m   5 m

12 m

b

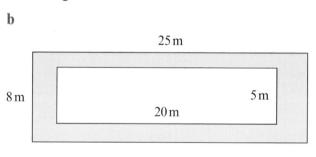

25 m

8 m   5 m

20 m

16 Calculate the coloured areas of these diagrams in square millimetres.

a

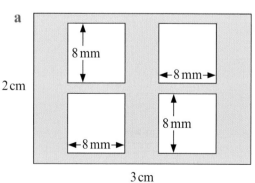

8 mm

←8 mm→

2 cm

←8 mm→

8 mm

3 cm

b

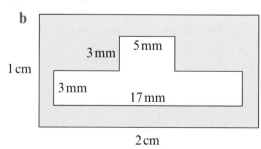

5 mm

3 mm

1 cm

3 mm

17 mm

2 cm

explanation 5

17 Find the area of each triangle.

a

9 cm
6 cm

b

11 cm
4 cm

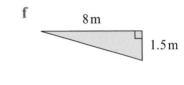

c

12 cm
12 cm

d

2 cm
13 cm

e

6 m
7 m

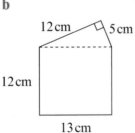

f

8 m
1.5 m

18 Work out the areas of these shapes.

a

20 m
10 m
11 m

b

12 cm
5 cm
12 cm
13 cm

c

6 cm
16 cm
7 cm
4 cm

explanation 6

19 The diagram shows an outline map of
the Isle of Man on a square grid. Each
square of the grid has an area of $25 \, km^2$.

Use the grid to estimate the area of the
Isle of Man.

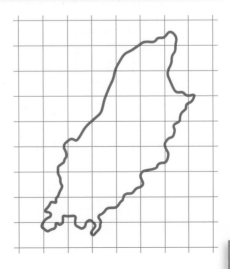

45

20 Diagram 1 shows a map of Loch Ness with a rectangle drawn around it.

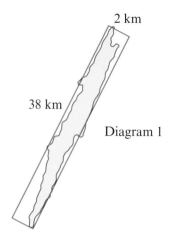

2 km

38 km

Diagram 1

a Use the diagram to estimate the area of the loch.

b Do you think that your estimate is more or less than the true area? Explain.

c Diagram 2 shows the loch again, but with some extra rectangles and triangles marked.
Removing these areas from the area of the large rectangle will give you an improved estimate of the area of the loch.

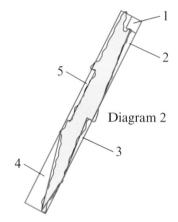

Diagram 2

i Copy and complete the table.

Number	Shape	Base (km)	Height (km)	Area (km²)
1	Rectangle	1	1.5	
2	Triangle	0.5	12	
3	Triangle	0.5	10	
4	Triangle	1.5	12	
5	Rectangle	8	0.5	
			Total	

ii What is your improved estimate of the area of Loch Ness?

Order of operations

- Working out calculations that involve more than one operation
- Working out calculations that involve squares and square roots
- Working out calculations that involve brackets

Keywords

You should know

explanation 1

1 Work out each of these calculations.

a $12 + 9 + 8$ b $16 - 3 - 11$ c $4 \times 5 \times 6$

d $50 \div 5 \div 5$ e $200 \div 2 \div 10$ f $3 \times 10 \times 10$

2 Work out the following calculations.

a $16 \times 2 \div 4$ b $40 \div 4 \times 7$ c $27 - 11 + 30$

d $19 + 6 - 12 + 9$ e $2 \times 2 \times 2 \times 2$ f $81 \div 3 \div 3 \div 3$

3 Copy and complete.

a $\square \times 3 \times 2 = 24$ b $\square \div 2 \div 5 = 12$ c $\square \times 100 \div 20 = 35$

d $48 \div \square \times 3 = 36$ e $427 - \square - 99 = 327$ f $1000 \div \square \div 5 = 8$

explanation 2

4 Work these out.

a $4 + 6 \times 3$ b $24 - 3 \times 7$ c $20 - 7 + 3 \times 4$

d $11 - 21 \div 3$ e $12 \div 4 + 36 \div 9$ f $6 \times 8 - 4 \times 12$

g $3 + 11 \times 2 - 9$ h $5 \times 4 - 18 \div 6$ i $4 + 7 - 40 \div 5$

5 Copy and complete these calculations using the correct operations.

a $5 \square 7 \times 2 = 19$ b $21 \square 3 + 11 = 18$ c $18 + 6 \square 2 = 21$

d $12 \square 2 \square 4 \times 5 = 26$ e $45 \square 15 \square 2 - 11 = 4$ f $24 \square 8 \square 5 = 15$

---

explanation 3

6 Work out each total.

a $3 + 5^2$

b 2×3^2

c $4^2 + 5^2$

d $100 - 7^2$

e $12 - \sqrt{16}$

f $\sqrt{25} + \sqrt{100}$

g $26 - 2 \times \sqrt{81}$

h $6^2 - 5 \times \sqrt{49}$

i $8^2 + 3 \times 10^2$

7 Use each of the numbers 5, 7 and 9 once to build the calculation below. Find the largest value that can be made.

$\square + \square \times \square^2$

---

explanation 4

8 Find each value.

a $17 - (21 - 10)$

b $3 \times (6 + 5)$

c $(10 - 3)^2$

d $4 \times (2 + 6)^2$

e $\sqrt{(9 + 5 \times 8)}$

f $16 - 5 \times (31 - 28)$

g $\sqrt{(3^2 + 4^2)}$

h $42 \div (5^2 - 6 \times 3)$

i $(9 + 11) \times (50 - 9 \times 5)$

9 Rewrite these statements and put in brackets where needed to make them true.

a $5 \times 4 + 3 = 35$

b $98 + 10 \div 12 = 9$

c $44 - 26 - 3 + 8 = 7$

d $48 \div 16 - 4 = 4$

e $7 + 24 \div 3 + 5 = 10$

f $11 + 21 \div 7 + 9 = 2$

g $18 \div 3 \times 2 = 3$

h $\sqrt{17} - 8 + 10 = 13$

i $\sqrt{25} + 5 \times 3 - 4 = 6$

---

explanation 5a   explanation 5b

10 Write each set of instructions as a calculation. You don't have to work it out. The first one is done for you.

a Add the square of 17 to 4 and find the square root.   Answer: $\sqrt{4 + 17^2}$

b Divide the sum of 75 and 45 by 12.

c Divide the sum of 57 and 96 by the sum of 38 and 53.

d Add 67.2 to 19.9, multiply the answer by 8 and subtract from 1000.

e Divide the square root of the sum of the squares of 11 and 15 by 28.

f Square the sum of 4.9 and 7.38 and divide the answer by 9.

Using a calculator (1)

- Using your calculator for complex calculations
- Using the calculator memory
- Checking calculator answers by estimation

Keywords

You should know

explanation 1

1 Work these out without a calculator. Then check your answers with a calculator.

 a $7 + 5 \times 2$ b $25 - 3 \times 8$ c $14 + 7 - 3 \times 5$

 d $18 \div 3 + 22 \div 11$ e $37 - 44 \div 4 + 21 \div 3$ f $48 \div 3 \div 8$

2 Use a calculator to work out the following calculations.

 a $37.2 - 7 \times 4.9$ b $12.8 + 9.4 \times 8$ c $11.3 - 9.8 + 7.2 \times 6$

 d $67.8 - 35.7 \div 7$ e $46.2 \div 3 + 71.1 \div 9$ f $18.6 + 11 \times 9.2 - 45.3$

3 Use the $\boxed{x^2}$ key on your calculator to find the value of these calculations.

 a 3.9^2 b 12.8^2 c 6.72^2

 d $50 - 6.8^2$ e $8.4^2 + 6.5^2$ f $21.6^2 - 19.9^2$

4 Use the $\boxed{\sqrt{}}$ key on your calculator to find the value of these calculations.

 a $\sqrt{70.56}$ b $\sqrt{151.29}$ c $\sqrt{376.36}$

 d $11.7 + \sqrt{210.25}$ e $\sqrt{353.44} - 7.69$ f $10 \times \sqrt{34.4569}$

5 Use the $\boxed{x^2}$ and $\boxed{\sqrt{}}$ keys on your calculator to work out these calculations.

 a $2.4^2 - \sqrt{31.36}$ b $5 \times \sqrt{2.89} + 1.6^2$

 c $7 \times 2.76^2 + 4.5^2$ d $3.09^2 - 2 \times \sqrt{16}$

 e $3 \times \sqrt{3.61} - 2 \times \sqrt{7.29}$ f $1.7 \times 1.56^2 - 3.2 \times \sqrt{1.5625}$

explanation 2

6 Use brackets on your calculator to find the value of each of these calculations.

a $6.4 \times (12.8 - 7.95)$

b $(3.7 + 5.4)^2$

c $32 - 4.8 \times (7.6 - 1.9)$

d $(18.6 + 19.7) \div 5$

e $29 \div (6.72 + 3.28)$

f $(2.3 + 6.9) \times (3.8 + 4.7)$

7 Use your calculator and insert brackets where necessary to work out these.

a $\sqrt{73.95 + 22.09}$

b $\dfrac{83.2}{4.7 + 8.1}$

c $\sqrt{300 - 17.76}$

d $\dfrac{89.94 + 41.92}{3.8}$

e $\dfrac{179.01}{2.6 \times 4.5}$

f $11 \times \sqrt{15.21}$

g $\dfrac{44.5 + \sqrt{20.25}}{9.8}$

h $\dfrac{8.7^2 - 5.3^2}{8.7 - 5.3}$

8 Work these out and round your answers to the nearest whole number.

a $5.87 + 7.9 \times 6.3$

b 4.87^2

c $\sqrt{11.92}$

d $450 - 9 \times (2.7 + 11.8)$

e $\sqrt{11^2 + 12^2}$

f 4×2.35^2

9 Work these out to the nearest pound.

a £68.51 × 1.175

b £428.56 × 0.175

c £3211 ÷ 7

d 8 × £43.24 + 17 × £16.35

e £500 − 2.4 × £98.76

f 36 × (£1.97 + 85p)

10 Work these out to the nearest kilogram.

a 17 × 5.648 kg

b 12 × 4.38 kg − 18 kg

c $\dfrac{16.6 \,\text{kg} + 18.2 \,\text{kg} + 5.4 \,\text{kg}}{3}$

d $(18 - 2.3) \times 4.8 \,\text{kg}$

explanation 3

11 A group of students returns from holiday with some American dollars. The bank will pay them £0.503 042 for each dollar. Calculate how much they receive to the nearest penny on the following amounts of money.

a $147

b $28

c $89

d $63

e $185

f $96

Use the memory keys to help you.

12 Pete the plumber has to work out how much VAT he has charged his customers. He does this by multiplying each bill total by 0.148 936 17.

Find the amount of VAT that Pete has included in these amounts to the nearest penny.

a £2782.40

b £1015.20

c £1373.58

d £899.27

e £571.96

f £3417.59

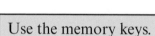

Use the memory keys.

explanation 4

13 Copy and complete to find estimates.

In each case, state whether the actual answer is more or less than your estimate.

a $20.657 + 3.869 \approx 21 + \square = \square$

b $9.8734 \times 14.910\,79 \approx 10 \times \square = \square$

c $8.192\,43^2 \approx \square^2 = \square$

d $\sqrt{84.348\,21} \approx \sqrt{\square} = \square$

14 Some of these calculations show incorrect answers. Use estimation to find out which are incorrect. Use a calculator to work out the actual answers.

a $4.768 \times 9.976 = 87.565\,568$

b $7.1489^2 = 51.106\,771\,21$

c $3127 + 4865 + 8076 + 2998 = 17\,366$

d $\sqrt{47.987} = 7.136\,587\,4$

e $(5.738 + 10.279)^2 = 256.544\,289$

f $129.7836 \div 25 = 5.191\,344$

Fractions and decimals

- Expressing one quantity as a fraction of another
- Using equivalent fractions
- Changing between improper fractions and mixed numbers
- Writing fractions as decimals

Keywords

You should know

explanation 1

1 Each of these shapes is divided into smaller parts of equal size.

   a Write the fraction of each shape that is coloured blue.

    i   **ii**   **iii**

    iv   **v**   **vi**

   b Write the fraction of each shape that is not coloured blue.

2 Two shapes are shown below. Each one has one part out of three coloured red. Does either shape have $\frac{1}{3}$ coloured red? Explain your answer.

Shape A   Shape B

3 Use the numbered scales to find the fraction of each of these rectangles that is green.

   a 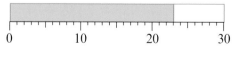   **b**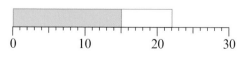

   c    **d**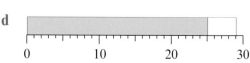

4   Write the first number as a fraction of the second for each of these pairs.

   a 16, 25   b 9, 11   c 42, 53

   d 73, 90   e 17, 30   f 3, 100

explanation 2a   explanation 2b

5 For each diagram, find a pair of equivalent fractions that show how much of the diagram is coloured purple.

a    b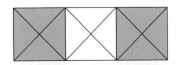

c 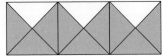   d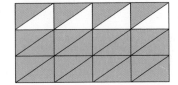

6 Copy and complete.

   a $\dfrac{2}{3} = \dfrac{10}{\square}$ b $\dfrac{4}{7} = \dfrac{\square}{21}$ c $\dfrac{3}{8} = \dfrac{12}{\square}$

   d $\dfrac{4}{5} = \dfrac{8}{\square} = \dfrac{\square}{25}$ e $\dfrac{3}{10} = \dfrac{\square}{30} = \dfrac{27}{\square}$ f $\dfrac{5}{6} = \dfrac{35}{\square} = \dfrac{\square}{54}$

7 Copy and complete.

   a $\dfrac{21}{28} = \dfrac{3}{\square}$ b $\dfrac{35}{45} = \dfrac{\square}{9}$ c $\dfrac{50}{75} = \dfrac{2}{\square}$

   d $\dfrac{44}{88} = \dfrac{22}{\square} = \dfrac{\square}{2}$ e $\dfrac{36}{48} = \dfrac{9}{\square} = \dfrac{\square}{4}$ f $\dfrac{60}{\square} = \dfrac{20}{30} = \dfrac{2}{\square}$

8 Write each of these fractions in their lowest terms.

   a $\dfrac{45}{90}$ b $\dfrac{55}{77}$ c $\dfrac{54}{72}$

   d $\dfrac{72}{240}$ e $\dfrac{225}{250}$ f $\dfrac{324}{396}$

9 Write $\dfrac{108}{144}$ in its simplest form.

explanation 3a   explanation 3b

10 You can use a fraction wall to compare fractions.

Use the fraction wall to help you. Copy and complete each statement, using < or >.

a $\frac{2}{7} \square \frac{1}{3}$ b $\frac{3}{5} \square \frac{4}{7}$

c $\frac{2}{3} \square \frac{7}{8}$ d $\frac{3}{8} \square \frac{2}{5}$

e $\frac{4}{5} \square \frac{6}{7}$ f $\frac{5}{6} \square \frac{2}{3}$

| $\frac{1}{8}$ | $\frac{1}{8}$ | $\frac{1}{8}$ | $\frac{1}{8}$ | $\frac{1}{8}$ | $\frac{1}{8}$ | $\frac{1}{8}$ | $\frac{1}{8}$ |

| $\frac{1}{7}$ | $\frac{1}{7}$ | $\frac{1}{7}$ | $\frac{1}{7}$ | $\frac{1}{7}$ | $\frac{1}{7}$ | $\frac{1}{7}$ |

| $\frac{1}{6}$ | $\frac{1}{6}$ | $\frac{1}{6}$ | $\frac{1}{6}$ | $\frac{1}{6}$ | $\frac{1}{6}$ |

| $\frac{1}{5}$ | $\frac{1}{5}$ | $\frac{1}{5}$ | $\frac{1}{5}$ | $\frac{1}{5}$ |

| $\frac{1}{4}$ | $\frac{1}{4}$ | $\frac{1}{4}$ | $\frac{1}{4}$ |

| $\frac{1}{3}$ | $\frac{1}{3}$ | $\frac{1}{3}$ |

| $\frac{1}{2}$ | $\frac{1}{2}$ |

11 Write these groups of fractions in order of size, smallest first. Use the fraction wall.

a $\frac{1}{2}, \frac{1}{3}, \frac{2}{5}$ b $\frac{3}{5}, \frac{4}{7}, \frac{5}{8}$ c $\frac{3}{4}, \frac{5}{6}, \frac{5}{7}$

d $\frac{7}{8}, \frac{6}{7}, \frac{3}{4}, \frac{5}{6}$ e $\frac{1}{2}, \frac{4}{7}, \frac{3}{8}, \frac{2}{5}$ f $\frac{2}{3}, \frac{4}{7}, \frac{3}{5}, \frac{5}{8}$

12 Write each pair of fractions with a common denominator. State which is the smaller.

a $\frac{5}{12}, \frac{9}{20}$ b $\frac{7}{10}, \frac{11}{15}$ c $\frac{3}{8}, \frac{5}{12}$

d $\frac{9}{16}, \frac{13}{24}$ e $\frac{4}{25}, \frac{16}{75}$ f $\frac{25}{27}, \frac{17}{18}$

explanation 4

13 Write these improper fractions as mixed numbers.

a $\frac{7}{3}$ b $\frac{11}{4}$ c $\frac{24}{5}$ d $\frac{31}{8}$ e $\frac{45}{11}$ f $\frac{99}{10}$

14 Write these mixed numbers as improper fractions.

a $4\frac{2}{3}$ b $2\frac{1}{5}$ c $6\frac{3}{4}$ d $9\frac{1}{2}$ e $7\frac{4}{5}$ f $5\frac{8}{9}$

15 Give your answers to these divisions as proper fractions in their lowest terms.

a $4 \div 6$ b $9 \div 12$ c $14 \div 20$ d $15 \div 18$

e $24 \div 30$ f $25 \div 75$ g $50 \div 75$ h $48 \div 60$

16 Give your answers to these divisions as mixed numbers in their simplest form.

a $18 \div 5$ b $30 \div 4$ c $24 \div 10$ d $21 \div 14$

e $50 \div 8$ f $11 \div 6$ g $40 \div 32$ h $250 \div 150$

| explanation 5 |

17 Write these decimals as fractions in their lowest terms.

a 0.3   b 0.1   c 0.7   d 0.9

e 0.5   f 0.25   g 0.75   h 0.8

i 0.24   j 0.35   k 0.6   l 0.55

18 a Copy and complete.

i $\dfrac{1}{5} = \dfrac{\square}{10}$ ii $\dfrac{2}{5} = \dfrac{\square}{10}$ iii $\dfrac{7}{20} = \dfrac{\square}{100}$ iv $\dfrac{11}{25} = \dfrac{\square}{100}$

v $\dfrac{9}{20} = \dfrac{\square}{100}$ vi $\dfrac{3}{50} = \dfrac{\square}{100}$ vii $\dfrac{49}{50} = \dfrac{\square}{100}$ viii $\dfrac{18}{75} = \dfrac{\square}{25} = \dfrac{\square}{100}$

b Write each fraction in part **a** as a decimal.

19 Write each fraction as a decimal.

a $\dfrac{19}{20}$ b $\dfrac{7}{25}$ c $\dfrac{27}{60}$ d $\dfrac{126}{200}$

20 Write each set of numbers in order of size, smallest first.

a $\dfrac{3}{4}$ 0.7   0.59 $\dfrac{1}{2}$ b $\dfrac{27}{50}$ 0.62   0.575 $\dfrac{3}{4}$ c 0.8 $\dfrac{7}{10}$ $\dfrac{15}{20}$ 0.72

21 Copy the number line. Show the output for this function machine on your number line.

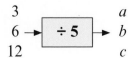

Percentages

- Representing a percentage on a diagram
- Converting between fractions, decimals and percentages

Keywords

You should know

explanation 1a   explanation 1b

1 Each diagram contains 100 squares. Answer the questions for each diagram.

   i   What fraction of the squares are yellow?

   ii What percentage of the squares are yellow?

   iii What fraction of the squares are not yellow?

   iv What percentage of the squares are not yellow?

a 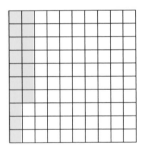   b 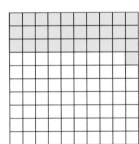   c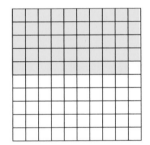

2 Copy and complete these statements.

   a $\dfrac{32}{100} = \square\%$

   b $\dfrac{44}{100} = \square\%$

   c $\dfrac{\square}{100} = 9\%$

   d $\dfrac{8}{10} = \dfrac{\square}{100} = \square\%$

   e $\dfrac{7}{20} = \dfrac{\square}{100} = \square\%$

   f $\dfrac{11}{25} = \dfrac{\square}{100} = \square\%$

   g $\dfrac{19}{50} = \dfrac{\square}{100} = \square\%$

   h $\dfrac{124}{200} = \dfrac{\square}{100} = \square\%$

   i $\dfrac{24}{300} = \dfrac{\square}{100} = \square\%$

3 28% of a diagram is coloured red.
   What percentage of the diagram is not coloured red?

4 A netball team has won 63% of its matches and drawn a further 18%.
   What percentage of matches has the netball team lost?

5 i What fraction of each diagram is white?

ii What percentage of each diagram is white?

a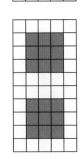

b

c

d

e

f

6 Compare your answers for question **3** parts **a**, **b** and **c** with those for **d**, **e** and **f**.

Explain any connection that you find.

7 a Here are two tiling patterns. What percentage
of each pattern is coloured grey?

i   **ii**

b The two tiling patterns from part **a** are combined
to make this pattern. What percentage of this
pattern is coloured grey?

c The pattern from part **b** is now repeated to make the complete mosaic
pattern below. What percentage of the mosaic is coloured grey?

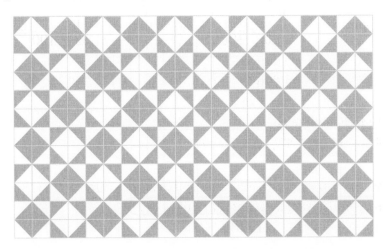

8 Use equivalent fractions to write each of these as a percentage.

a $\dfrac{1}{2}$ b $\dfrac{1}{4}$ c $\dfrac{1}{5}$ d $\dfrac{1}{10}$ e $\dfrac{3}{4}$ f $\dfrac{4}{5}$

9 Use equivalent fractions to write each of these as a percentage.

a $\dfrac{7}{25}$ b $\dfrac{11}{20}$ c $\dfrac{27}{50}$

d $\dfrac{7}{10}$ e $\dfrac{162}{200}$ f $\dfrac{240}{400}$

g $\dfrac{63}{75}$ h $\dfrac{45}{60}$ i $\dfrac{30}{125}$

10 Write each percentage as a fraction and simplify where possible.

a   60%   b   29%   c   80%

d   45%   e   32%   f   70%

g   7%   h   84%   i   12.5%

11 Copy the diagram and shade 35% of it.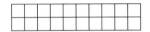

12 Copy these diagrams and shade the percentage shown.

a

36%

b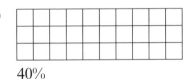

40%

c

65%

d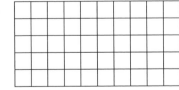

28%

e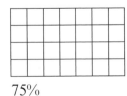

75%

f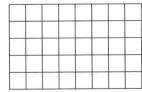

12.5%

explanation 2

13 Write these fractions and percentages as decimals.

   a $\dfrac{23}{100}$ b $\dfrac{9}{100}$ c 47%

   d 8%   e 50%   f 25%

   g 86%   h 12.5%   i 17.5%

   j 14.8%   k 3.5%   l 6.3%

14 Write these decimals as percentages.

   a 0.39   b 0.75   c 0.06

   d 0.01   e 0.275   f 0.375

   g 0.764   h 0.083   i 0.108

15 Copy and complete the table.

	Fraction	Decimal	Percentage
a		0.4	
b	$\dfrac{7}{20}$		
c		0.95	
d			65
e	$\dfrac{12}{25}$		
f			72
g	$\dfrac{11}{50}$		
h			35

16 Write these numbers in order of size, smallest first.

   66%, 0.085, $\dfrac{7}{10}$, 57.9%, $\dfrac{17}{20}$

Working with data

- Finding the mean, median and mode
- Finding the range

You should know

explanation 1

1 Find the mode of each set of data.

  a 7, 11, 10, 7, 9, 10, 7, 12, 9

  b 18, 24, 21, 20, 23, 21, 18, 21, 22

  c 5 m, 3 m, 4 m, 6 m, 3 m, 6 m, 8 m, 6 m, 5 m, 6 m, 8 m, 3 m, 5 m, 6 m, 7 m

  d red, blue, yellow, blue, yellow, green, blue, red, blue, yellow, red, blue, white

  e bus, car, car, walk, bus, car, bus, walk, walk, bus, car, cycle, car, walk, cycle

2 There are 31 pupils in class 7N. The table below shows the number of absences recorded for the class in one week.

Number of absences	0	1	2	3	4
Number of pupils	24	3	2	0	

  a How many pupils were absent on four occasions?

  b What is the modal number of absences?

3 This bar chart shows the results of a survey of pupils' favourite school dinners.

  a How many pupils took part in the survey?

  b What is the mode?

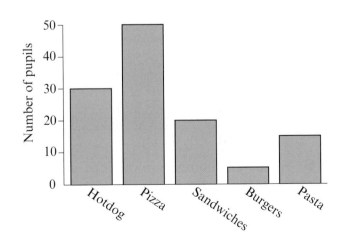

4 The results of two traffic surveys of 100 vehicles are shown in the tables below.

One survey involved early morning motorway traffic on a weekday.

The other survey involved vehicles approaching the Dover ferry on a Saturday.

Table 1

Number of people in vehicle	1	2	3	4	More than 4
Number of vehicles	12	28	35		11

Table 2

Number of people in vehicle	1	2	3	4	More than 4
Number of vehicles		21	15	5	3

a Find the missing value in each table.

b What is the mode for each survey?

c Which survey do you think Table 1 represents? Explain how you made your decision.

5 This set of data has two modal values. Find them.

52, 49, 55, 51, 52, 51, 49, 57, 55, 53, 57, 52, 49, 55, 56, 49, 54, 55, 51

explanation 2

6 The pulse rates of 60 pupils are shown below.

65 48 79 76 53 91 64 93 87 89 74 58
69 83 75 59 48 76 78 69 82 93 68 57
49 62 70 75 74 92 65 79 84 77 92 75
54 71 68 73 58 76 57 90 68 89 70 56
87 75 51 61 55 70 77 63 75 78 86 70

a Copy and complete the frequency table.

Pulse rate	41–50	51–60	61–70	71–80	81–90	91–100
Tally						
Frequency						

b Which is the modal class?

c What percentage of the pupils are in the modal class?

7 a Find the mode of this set of numbers.

18, 15, 20, 16, 15, 20, 18, 16, 20

b Do you think that the mode is typical of the data in this case? Explain your answer.

c Choose a value that you think is more typical of the data.

Describe how you made your choice.

8 These are the times in minutes that seven people waited at a doctor's surgery.

1   5   6   7   10   11   15

a Explain why the mode is not a suitable average in this case.

b Choose a value that you think is typical of the data.

Describe how you made your choice.

explanation 3

9

| 1.38 m | 1.41 m | 1.45 m | 1.49 m | 1.52 m |

What is the median height of this group of friends?

10 Find the median of each set of numbers.

a 4   4   4   5   6   6   7   8   8

b 7.2   7.5   7.5   7.6   7.6   7.8   7.8   7.8   7.9   7.9   7.9

c 16   16   17   18   18   18   19   19

d 21   23   24   27   29   29   30   30

e 9   9   10   10   10   11   11   12   12   12

> Remember to put
> the data in order
> of size first.

11 Find the median of each set of numbers.

    a   32   37   28   31   33   29   33   37   32

    b   24   19   25   23   25   20   26   19   27   23   24

    c   1.6   1.4   1.2   0.9   1.3   1.2   1.4   1.5   1.3   1.2   1.0   0.9   1.1

    d   53   47   55   48   59   56   49   50   47   54

    e   2.5   2   2.7   2.7   2.9   2.5   2.6   2.8   2.5   2.78

12 The pupils in one class said how much time they spend on homework each
week. The results are shown in the bar charts below.

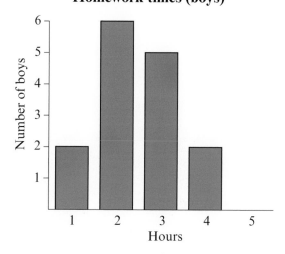

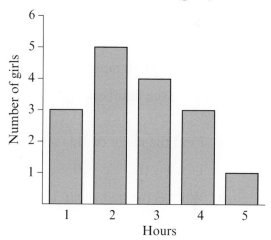

    a   Use the boys chart to list their times in order.

    b   Find the median time that the boys spend on homework.

    c   Use the girls chart to list their times in order.

    d   Find the median time that the girls spend on homework.

13   **a**   Write down the value of the median for this set of numbers.

        3   6   9   10   24   48   96

    b   Do you think that the median is typical of the data in this case?
       Explain your answer.

    c   What happens to the median if the 48 is replaced with 76?

    d   Explain why the mode cannot be used here.

explanation 4a   explanation 4b

14 Work out the mean of each set of numbers.

a 5   4   4   3   6   8

b 120   95   115

c 6.8   9.3   7.6   8.7   7.6

d 21   27   25   22   23   24   21   20   25   22

e 6   8   7   9   11   8   5   9   7   12

15 a Find the mean of this set of numbers.

7   9   3   4   6

b Find the new mean if the 3 is replaced by 4.

16 The mean of 10 numbers is 2.76.

What do the numbers add up to?

17 a Find the mean of this set of numbers.

1   3   6   2   0

b What is the new mean if each number is increased by 1?

c What is the new mean if each number is doubled?

18 The mean of these numbers is 4.

3.8   2.7   ☐   5.1   5.3

What is the value of the missing number?

19 The three sides of this triangle have a mean length of 10 cm.
Find the length of side AC.

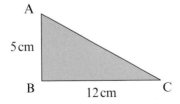

20 Use a calculator to find the mean of each set of data.

Where necessary, round your answers to 1 decimal place.

a 47   63   58   49   65   72

b 14   12   17   21   18   19   13   20   16   15   18

c 18.3 cm   14.6 cm   13.9 cm   17.8 cm   19.3 cm   16.9 cm   14.8 cm

d 7.8 kg   4.3 kg   6.1 kg   7.2 kg   8.7 kg   9.8 kg   8.5 kg   6.7 kg

21 These are the prices of some studio apartments in Spain.

€140 000   €147 000   €138 000   €152 000   €164 000

Find the mean cost of these studio apartments to the nearest €1000.

22 The mean of 7 numbers is 12.8.

One of the numbers is removed. Find its value if:

a the mean is reduced to 11.7   **b** the mean is unchanged

c the mean increases to 12.9

explanation 5

23 The youth club football team played 12 matches last season.

The table shows the number of goals that they scored.

Goals scored per match G	Number of matches N	G × N
0	1	
1	4	
2	3	6
3	2	
4	2	
	Total =	Total =

a Copy the table and fill in the missing values.

b Copy and complete:

mean number of goals per match = $\dfrac{\text{total number of ...}}{\text{total number of ...}} = \dfrac{\square}{\square}$

24 Tickets for a theatre performance of The Lion King were sold at three prices. The table shows the number of tickets sold at each price for one performance.

Ticket price T	Number of tickets sold N	T × N
£28.50	396	
£38.50	180	
£48.50	164	
	Total =	Total =

a Copy the table and fill in the missing values.

b Calculate the mean price paid per ticket to the nearest penny.

$$\text{Mean price paid per ticket} = \frac{\text{total cost of} \ldots}{\text{total number of} \ldots} = \frac{\square}{\square}$$

25 Mr Brown keeps a record of the number of merit slips awarded to the pupils in his class for good work. This table shows the number of merits awarded in one day.

Merit slips awarded M	Number of pupils N	M × N
0	6	
1	4	
2	10	
3	7	
4	2	
	Total =	Total =

a How many pupils are there in Mr Brown's class?

b How many merit slips were awarded that day?

c Use a calculator to work out the mean number of merit slips per pupil to 1 decimal place.

d On the same day the previous week, the mean was 1.6 to 1 decimal place.

Did Mr Brown's class perform better or worse than the previous week?

e What if Mr Brown had only calculated the means to the nearest whole number?

26 Sophie threw a dice 100 times and recorded the scores. This table shows her results.

Score S	Frequency F	... × ...
1	11	
2	17	
3	18	
4	14	
5	19	
6		
Total =		Total =

a How many 6s did Sophie throw?

b Copy and complete the table.

c Calculate Sophie's mean score per throw.

27 These are the hourly rates of pay for seven workers at a small company.

£6.80 £7.30 £6.20 £6.60 £6.20 £30 £6.90

a Work out the mean hourly rate.

b Do you think that the mean is a good average to use here? Explain your answer.

c Find the median and the mode. Which type of average is most typical of the data?

explanation 6

28 Find the range of each set of data.

a 24 32 31 19 21 25 20 29

b 4.7 4.8 3.6 5.1 4.7 3.8 5.4

c 9 cm 11 cm 6 cm 12 cm 14 cm 13 cm 10 cm

d 28.4 m^2 27.6 m^2 24.9 m^2 26.7 m^2 29.9 m^2

29 The tallest person in Luke's class has a height of 1.6 m.

The range of the heights is 0.18 m.

What is the height of the shortest person in Luke's class?

30 The range of these numbers is 5.4.

11.3   ☐   12.7   9.1   13.6

What are the two possible values of the missing number?

31 The mode of these numbers is 9.2. What is their range?

9.7   9.8   9.2   9.8   ☐   9.6   9.2

32 The range of these numbers is 11 and their median is 124.

124   132   ☐   123   125

What is the missing number?

33 **a** Write down 5 numbers with a range of 0.5 and a median of 16.

b Copy and complete the following statements using the highlighted words below.

i If the range of a set of numbers is very small then ...

ii If the range of a set of numbers is large then ...

all of the numbers must be far apart

all of the numbers must be close together

not all of the numbers can be close together

34 Here are some numbers.   4   6   9   10   12

a Which one should you reduce by 2 to increase the range?

b Which one can you increase by 3 without affecting the median or the range?

c Which one should you reduce by 1 to make the mean, the median and the range have the same value?

Representing data

- Interpreting various types of chart used in statistics
- Drawing a bar chart
- Drawing a frequency diagram for grouped data

Keywords

You should know

explanation 1

1 This pictogram shows how many people attended a school play.

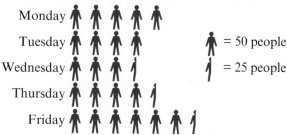

Number of people attending the school play

Monday

Tuesday

Wednesday

Thursday

Friday

🏃 = 50 people

🏃 = 25 people

a How many people attended the play on these days?

   i Monday   **ii** Thursday

b Which day was the most popular?

c What is the range of the attendance figures?

d How many people went to the play altogether?

2 The table shows the highest speeds reached by some rides at Alton Towers.
Draw a bar-line graph to show this information.

Ride	Speed (mph)
Air	46
Beastie	9
Corkscrew	40
Nemesis	50
Oblivion	68
Rita – Queen of speed	61
Runaway train	22

3 Internet search engines handle a huge number of enquiries every day. This bar-line graph shows some of the most popular enquiries on one particular day.

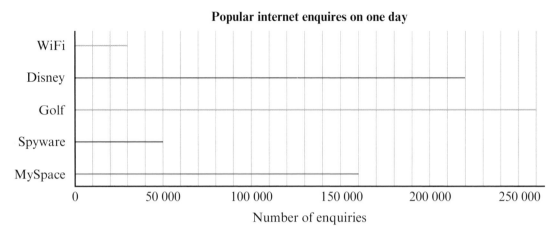

Popular internet enquires on one day

a How many enquires were there for Disney?

b Which enquiry was the mode?

c What is the total number of enquiries for the items shown?

(explanation 2a)   (explanation 2b)

4 This bar chart shows the percentage of regular smokers aged 11–15, according to a recent survey.

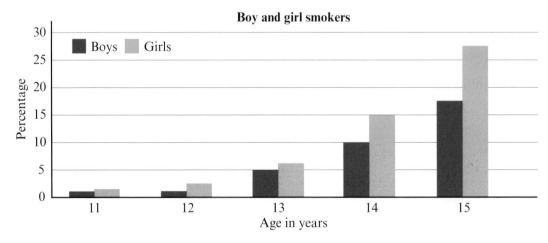

Boy and girl smokers

a What are the two key points that the chart shows?

b What is the increase in percentage of boys smoking from 12 to 15?

c What is the increase in percentage of girls smoking from 12 to 15?

5 A group of pupils was asked about things that they might do at some point in the future. This table shows their responses.

Draw a bar chart for the data.

To do	Boys %	Girls %
Learn to drive	100	90
Climb a mountain	67	35
Go to university	33	40
Get married	74	92
Bungee jump	44	55
Run a marathon	38	40

6 100 girls in primary schools and in secondary schools were asked to name their favourite subject. The bar chart shows the results.

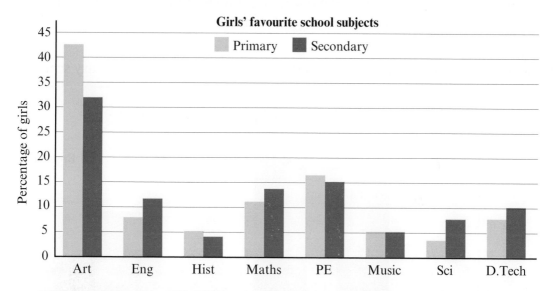

a Which subjects lost popularity from primary to secondary?

b Which subject maintained the same level of popularity?

c List the subjects in order of popularity at primary level.

d List the subjects in order of popularity at secondary level.

e Which subjects gained in popularity from primary to secondary?

7 The table shows the favourite subjects of 100 boys at primary level and 100 boys at secondary level.

Subject	Primary	Secondary
Art	35	20
English	5	7
History	6	4
Maths	11	15
PE	28	32
Music	3	3
Science	5	8
Design and Tech.	7	11

   a Draw a bar chart to represent this data.

   b Compare your chart to the one in question **6**. Which two subjects show the biggest difference between the girls and the boys?

8 This compound bar chart shows the music preferences of secondary school pupils.

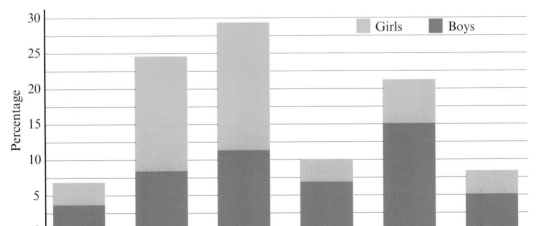

Music preferences of boys and girls

   a Overall, which type of music is the most popular?

   b Which type of music is most popular with boys?

   c Which two types of music do girls prefer?

explanation 3

9 A prize was offered at a school fair for the best estimate of the number of sweets in a large jar. The estimates were:

147	138	124	150	97	134	110	137
82	115	142	163	158	133	117	155
136	149	112	160	98	125	158	142
140	156	128	167	144	131	138	150
129	131	146	140	149	98	111	146
139	140	150	109	167	130	135	152

a Copy and complete the table using equal-sized class intervals.

Estimate	80–99	100–119			
Tally					
Frequency					

b Draw a frequency diagram to represent the data.

c What is the modal class?

d What is the range of the estimates?

e How many estimates were less than 140?

10 This table shows the number of Christmas raffle tickets sold by the pupils of 7T.

Number of tickets	1–5	6–10	11–15	16–20	21–25	26–30
Frequency	5	11	6	3	1	2

a Draw a frequency diagram to represent the data.

b What is the modal class?

c Explain why the range cannot be found exactly.

d There are 30 pupils in 7T. How many didn't sell any tickets?

e How many pupils sold more than 15 tickets? What percentage is this?

11 Earthworms are known to improve the quality of soil. The number of earthworms present in an area gives one measure of the quality of the soil. This table shows how the number of worms varied in an area of pasture.

Worms/m^2	100–199	200–299	300–399	400–499	500–599
Frequency	9	13	19	12	7

  a Draw a frequency diagram to represent the data.

  b What is the modal class?

  c Which class contains the median?

  d What percentage of the sample area contained less than 200 worms/m^2?

> explanation 4

12 This pie chart shows the favourite reading of a group of pupils.

  a What percentage of pupils chose Romance?

  b What was the modal choice?

  c If 26 pupils chose Fantasy, how many chose Crime?

Favourite books

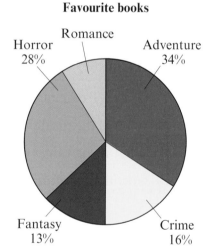

Romance
Horror 28%
Adventure 34%
Fantasy 13%
Crime 16%

13 This pie chart shows the mix of boys and girls who joined an after-school dance class.

  a What percentage of the class were boys?

  b If there were 27 girls in the class, how many pupils attended altogether?

Dance class members

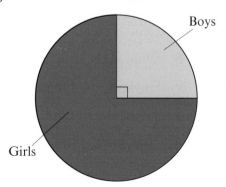

Boys

Girls

14 Equal numbers of boys and girls were asked how many cans of drink they had drunk in the last two days. These pie charts show the results.

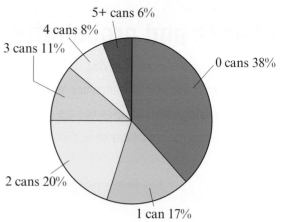

Cans drunk by boys

5+ cans 6%
4 cans 8%
3 cans 11%
0 cans 38%
2 cans 20%
1 can 17%

a Did more boys or girls drink 1 can in the last two days?

b Overall, did boys or girls drink the most cans?

c What is the modal number of cans drunk?

d 32 girls drank 2 cans in the last two days.

i How many boys drank 2 cans?

ii How many girls drank less than 2 cans?

iii How many boys drank more than 3 cans?

iv How many pupils took part?

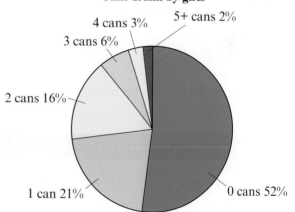

Cans drunk by girls

4 cans 3%
5+ cans 2%
3 cans 6%
2 cans 16%
1 can 21%
0 cans 52%

explanation 5

15 In 1982 the California Condor was on the brink of extinction. Between 1982 and 1987 the remaining 27 birds were captured. This line graph tells the story between 1987 and 2007.

a In 1992 some birds were re-introduced to the wild. How many?

b What was the total population of California Condors in 1997?

c Explain the dip in the captive population shown between 2002 and 2007.

d What was the total population in 2007?

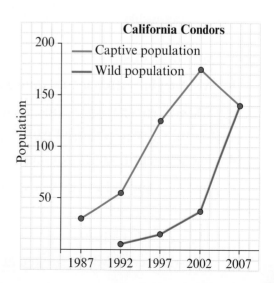

California Condors

— Captive population
— Wild population

Population

200
150
100
50

1987 1992 1997 2002 2007

Chance and probability

- Describing situations involving chance
- Identifying the possible outcomes for a situation
- Recognising when the outcomes are equally likely
- Calculating the probability of an event for equally likely outcomes

Keywords

You should know

explanation 1

1 The diagram shows a scale ranging from impossible to certain.

The letters a, b, c and d are positioned on this scale to match these labels.

| likely | unlikely | very unlikely | very likely |

Match the letters to the labels.

```
        a            b                    c       d
  ┌──────────────────────────────────────────────────┐
  │                                                    │
  └──────────────────────────────────────────────────┘
  Impossible               Even chance            Certain
```

2 Which of these labels best describes the likelihood of each event below?

| certain | impossible | likely | unlikely | very likely | very unlikely | even chance |

a You score more than 2 when you roll an ordinary dice.

b A stone thrown up into clear air will fall back down.

c You will correctly guess the answer to a multiple choice question with 3 options.

d The winner of a television quiz show is a woman.

e One day you will win the jackpot in the lottery.

f A monkey will spell out I LUV MATHS when playing with a keyboard.

g A world record will be broken at the next Olympics.

h You score 7 when you roll an ordinary dice.

3 Arrange these outcomes in order from the least likely to the most likely.

This spinner lands on blue.
A coin lands heads up.
This spinner lands on green.
A dice is rolled and gives a score of 3.

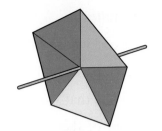

4 Describe the chances of these outcomes as better than even or less than even.

   a You correctly guess a person's favourite colour.

   b A learner driver passes their driving test on the first attempt.

   c At least one goal is scored in a selected football match.

   d The next person to enter the room is right-handed.

Around 43% of people pass their driving test first time.

> explanation 2

5 At the start of his mind-reading act, Alfonso turns his back on the audience and throws a teddy bear over his shoulder.

The person who catches the teddy bear is then invited onto the stage to take part in the act.

   a Why doesn't Alfonso just ask for a volunteer?

   b Why doesn't he face the audience to throw the teddy bear?

   c Do you think that selecting a person this way will give Alfonso any unfair advantage?

6 Here are some of the ways of selecting one person from a group of people.

- Pick the tallest.
- Pick the one whose surname is first alphabetically.
- Write each name on a piece of paper and choose one without looking.
- Pick the one that you like the most.

a Which one of these is the only way to select a person at random?

b What precaution would you take to make sure that the selection was fair?

7 A normal dice is rolled. List the outcomes for each of these events.

a An odd number is scored.

b A prime number is scored.

c The score is less than 5.

d The score is not less than 5.

e The score is greater than 5.

f At least 2 is scored.

8 A card is selected at random from these coloured digit cards.

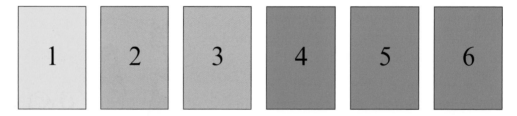

Write down the number of outcomes for these events.

a The number on the card is at least 4.

b The card is blue.

c The card is not yellow.

d The card is blue and the number is even.

e The card is not green and the number is odd.

f The number on the card is neither even nor prime.

explanation 3

9 **a** How many outcomes are there for this spinner?

   b How many of these outcomes are green?

   c Find the probability that the spinner lands on

   i green

   ii blue

   iii any number apart from 4

   iv a blue odd number.

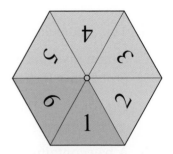

10 Find the probability that this spinner lands on

   a red

   b purple

   c either red or purple

   d any colour apart from red.

11 These counters are put into a bag and one is selected at random.

   a How many outcomes are there in total?

   b How many of the outcomes are red?

   c What is the probability that the counter selected is red?

   d How many of the outcomes are red or yellow?

   e What is the probability that the selected counter is red or yellow?

   f How many of the counters are green?

   g What is the probability that the selected counter is green?

12 **a** What is the probability of an event that is certain to happen?

   b What is the probability of an event that cannot happen?

13 Copy this probability scale and fill in the blank labels.

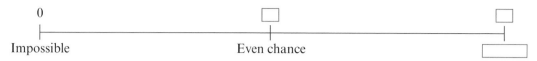

0   □   □

Impossible   Even chance

14 This triangular spinner has 3 possible outcomes.

Simon says that 1 outcome out of 3 is yellow so the probability that the spinner lands on yellow is $\frac{1}{3}$.

Do you think that Simon is right? Explain your answer.

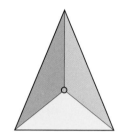

15 A bag contains 3 red counters and 2 blue counters. The counters are identical apart from their colour. One counter is selected at random.

    a Write the probability that the counter is red in three ways:

        i as a fraction   **ii** as a decimal   **iii** as a percentage

    b Write the probability that the counter is either red or blue as a percentage.

    c What is the probability that the counter is pink?

16 A bag contains 3 cabbages and 2 bars of chocolate. Katie can select one item from the bag without looking. John says that the probability that Katie selects a bar of chocolate is 40%.

    a How has John worked out his answer?

        Do you think he is right?

    b What do you think is a more realistic value?

17 The local weather forecast gives the probability that it will rain today as 25%.

What is the probability that it will not rain here today?

18 20% of the cars in a car park are red. One quarter of the cars are blue.

A car in the car park is selected at random.

    a What is the probability, as a fraction, that the car is red?

    b What is the probability, as a decimal, that the car is either red or blue?

    c What is the probability, as a percentage, that the car is neither red nor blue?

Formulae

- Using a formula
- Simplifying expressions in algebra
- Building and simplifying a formula

explanation 1a   explanation 1b

1 What is the value of each expression?

a $2 + 3 \times 4$ b $21 - 2 \times 9$ c $5(2 + 6)$

d $5 \times 2 + 6$ e $8 \times 6 - 3 \times 4$ f $8(6 - 3) \times 4$

g $3 \times 5 + 6 \times 4$ h $7 + 6 \div 2$ i $(7 + 6) \div 2$

j $10 \div 2 + 12 \div 3$ k $15 - 7 + 4$ l $15 - (7 + 4)$

2 What is the value of each expression?

a $3 \times 4 \times 5$ b $3 \times (4 \times 5)$ c $54 \div 6 \div 3$

d $54 \div (6 \div 3)$ e $18 - (10 - 6)$ f $18 - 10 - 6$

g $4 + 7 + 5$ h $4 + (7 + 5)$ i $9 + (7 - 3)$

j $9 + 7 - 3$ k $30 - 21 + 8$ l $30 - (21 + 8)$

3 Find the value of each expression when $x = 5$.

a $x + 3$ b $2x$ c $3x$

d $4x - 7$ e $10 - x$ f $27 - 2x$

g $15 - x + 3$ h $12 - x - 4$ i $4 - x$

j $-2x$ k $10 - 2x$ l $-2x + 10$

4 Find the value of each expression when $y = 3$.

a $3(y + 6)$ b $50 - 4(y + 1)$ c $12 + 2(y - 1)$

d $3(y + 2y)$ e $10 - 2(6 - y)$ f $3y - y$

g $(y - 2) + (7 - 2y)$ h $y - (2 - y)$ i $(y + 1) \times (y + 2)$

5 Find the value of each expression when $x = 12$.

a $\dfrac{x}{3}$

b $\dfrac{x+8}{4}$

c $\dfrac{x-3}{3}$

d $\dfrac{3x}{4}$

e $\dfrac{2x}{3}$

f $\dfrac{5x}{6}$

g $\dfrac{60}{x}$

h $\dfrac{108}{x}$

*i $\dfrac{18}{x-3}$

6 Find the value of each expression when $x = 7$ and $y = 4$.

a $x + y$

b $x - y$

c $x + 2y$

d $2x + y$

e $x + 3y$

f $20 - x - y$

g $3(x + y)$

h $2x + 5y$

i $5 - (x - y)$

j $\dfrac{x+1}{y}$

k $\dfrac{15}{x-y}$

l $\dfrac{42}{x} - y$

explanation 2a   explanation 2b

7 Simplify these expressions.

a $x + 2 + 3$

b $x + 9 - 2$

c $x + 3 \times 4$

d $x + x$

e $x + x + x$

f $x + x - x$

g $2x + x$

h $2x - x$

i $2x + 3x$

j $3x - 2x$

k $5x + 3x + x$

l $9x - 2x - 4x$

8 Copy and complete these expressions.

a $39 + 27 + 1 = 39 + 1 + \square = \square$

b $28 + 75 + 25 + 11 = 28 + \square + 11 = \square$

c $327 - 98 - 2 + 30 = 327 - \square + 30 = \square$

d $579 + 86 - 79 = 579 - \square + \square = \square$

e $49 + 78 + 51 + 65 + 22 = 49 + \square + 78 + \square + 65 = \square$

9 Explain what question **8** shows about addition and subtraction.

10 Work out these expressions by rewriting in the simplest order.

a 75 + 49 + 25 + 51 + 88

b 53 + 94 + 6 + 75 + 47

c 78 + 67 − 18 + 40

d 139 − 43 − 56 − 1

e 11 − 18 + 58 − 21

f 32 − 54 − 16 + 68

11 Simplify these expressions by rewriting to group togther like terms.

a $x + 3 + x$

b $x + 4 + x + 6$

c $2x + 5 + x - 3$

d $x + x - x + x - x$

e $5x - 3 - x + 7$

f $4 - 2x - 4 + 7x$

12 Simplify these expressions. Rewrite to group together like terms where necessary.

a $x + y + y$

b $2x - y + y$

c $3x + y - x + y$

d $x + 3 + y + 5$

e $x - y + y + x + 3$

f $2x + y - 3 - x + 4y$

g $xy + xy$

h $2xy + 3xy$

i $xyz + xyz$

j $3xy - 4y - 2yx$

k $2zyx - yx + 1 + xyz$

l $2 + p + pqr - 2 - 3pqr$

13 Write expressions for the following situations as simply as possible:

a Simon has $x + 3$ sweets.
Jo has 4 more sweets than Simon.
How many sweets does Jo have?

b Helen lives x miles away from school.
Jane lives a further y miles from school.
How many miles from school does Jane live?

c Rob has n marbles but loses 5 of them.
How many does he have left?

d Liz has p marbles but loses q of them.
How many does she have left?

14 Jack has k computer games and Jill has t computer games.
Jack swaps 3 of his games for 1 of Jill's.

a How many games does Jack then have?

b How many games does Jill have?

explanation 3

15 Find and simplify a formula for the perimeter, P, of each shape.

a

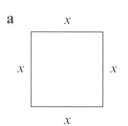

b

c

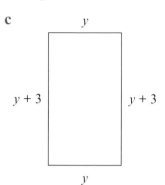

16 Find and simplify a formula for the perimeter, P, of each shape.

a

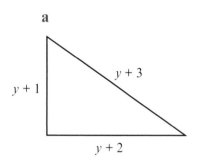

b

c

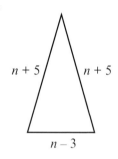

d

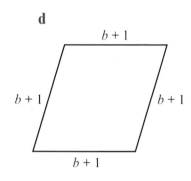

e

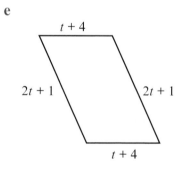

f

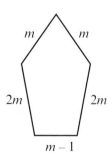

g

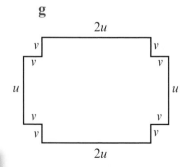

h

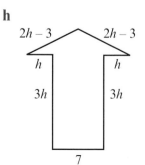

i

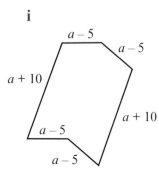

17

A
$$2x$$

B
$$x + 3$$

C
$$x - 5$$

D
$$7 - x$$

E
$$4 - 2x$$

F
$$3x + 1$$

a   Which two cards total $4x + 4$?

b   Which two cards total $x + 5$?

c   Which two cards total 4?

d   Which two cards total 10?

e   Which three cards total 12?

f   Which three cards total $3x + 11$?

g   What is the total of all of the expressions on the cards?

(explanation 4)

18 Use the formula $B = H + M$.

a   Find B when $H = 5$ and $M = 7$.

b   Find B when $H = 5$ and $M = 2$.

c   Find B when $H = 3.5$ and $M = 2$.

19 Use the formula $s = \dfrac{d}{t}$.

a   Find s when $d = 12$ and $t = 3$.

b   Find s when $d = 56$ and $t = 8$.

c   Find s when $d = 150$ and $t = 25$.

d   Find d when $s = 20$ and $t = 11$.

20 Use the formula $F = ma$.

a   Find F when $m = 3$ and $a = 10$.

b   Find F when $m = 4.8$ and $a = 10$.

c   Find F when $m = 5$ and $a = 1.3$.

d   Find m when $F = 24$ and $a = 4$.

21 Look at these diagrams.

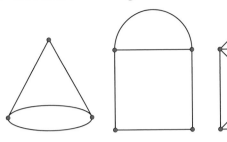

N	A	R
3	4	3

N represents the number of red dots.
A represents the number of arcs or lines.
R represents the number of regions or spaces.

The table shows the values of N, A and R for the first diagram. Notice that the outside of the diagram counts as a region, so $R = 3$.

a Copy and complete the table for the other two diagrams.

b Draw some diagrams of your own and fill in the table.

c Work out the value of $N + A - R$ for each row in the table.
What do you notice?
Copy and complete this formula:
$N + A - R = \square$.

22 Copy and complete the table using the formula $v = u + at$.

u	a	t	v
16	2.7	8	
11	5.6	7	
	3.5	12	50
30	6.7		164
45		4.6	79.5

23 Use the formula $d = \frac{m}{v}$ to find d to 2 d.p. for these values of m and v.

a $m = 50$ and $v = 41$

b $m = 220$ and $v = 176$

c $m = 350$ and $v = 423$

Functions and equations

- Representing an equation using a flow diagram
- Solving an equation using inverse operations

Keywords

You should know

explanation 1a explanation 1b

1 Write the output of each function machine.

a $5 \rightarrow \boxed{-3} \rightarrow$

b $12 \rightarrow \boxed{\div 3} \rightarrow$

c $3 \rightarrow \boxed{+7} \rightarrow$

d $0.5 \rightarrow \boxed{\times 2} \rightarrow$

e $7 \rightarrow \boxed{-7} \rightarrow$

f $-1 \rightarrow \boxed{+1} \rightarrow$

2 Write an expression for the output of each function machine.

a $x \rightarrow \boxed{+2} \rightarrow$

b $x \rightarrow \boxed{\div 3} \rightarrow$

c $x \rightarrow \boxed{\times 5} \rightarrow$

d $x \rightarrow \boxed{-9} \rightarrow$

e $y \rightarrow \boxed{-4} \rightarrow$

f $g \rightarrow \boxed{\times 8} \rightarrow$

g $t \rightarrow \boxed{+11} \rightarrow$

h $n \rightarrow \boxed{\div 5} \rightarrow$

3 Write an expression for the output of each function machine.

a $x \rightarrow \boxed{\times 6} \rightarrow \boxed{+5} \rightarrow$

b $x \rightarrow \boxed{\times 4} \rightarrow \boxed{-3} \rightarrow$

c $x \rightarrow \boxed{\div 3} \rightarrow \boxed{-7} \rightarrow$

d $x \rightarrow \boxed{\div 8} \rightarrow \boxed{+1} \rightarrow$

e $x \rightarrow \boxed{+4} \rightarrow \boxed{\times 5} \rightarrow$

f $x \rightarrow \boxed{-5} \rightarrow \boxed{\div 10} \rightarrow$

4 Draw a function machine to represent each expression.

a $2g + 7$

b $3(h - 9)$

c $4(t + 3)$

d $5r - 10$

e $\dfrac{x}{4} - 5$

f $\dfrac{m}{9} + 6$

g $\dfrac{f + 4}{2}$

h $\dfrac{k - 12}{7}$

5 Here are some reverse function machines. Write the value of x for each one.

a $x \leftarrow \boxed{+2} \leftarrow 8$ b $x \leftarrow \boxed{\div 3} \leftarrow 12$

c $x \leftarrow \boxed{+4} \leftarrow \boxed{\times 5} \leftarrow 7$ d $x \leftarrow \boxed{\div 9} \leftarrow \boxed{+7} \leftarrow 11$

6 Write the inverse of each operation.

a   Add 6   b   Multiply by 5   c   Subtract 1   d   Divide by 2

e $+5$ f $\times 6$ g $\div 3$ h -9

i $\times 10$ j $+3.4$ k -9.8 l $\div 7.2$

7 This function machine represents the equation $\frac{x}{4} - 5 = 6$.

$$x \rightarrow \boxed{\div 4} \rightarrow \boxed{-5} \rightarrow 6$$

a   Copy and complete the reverse function machine using inverse operations.

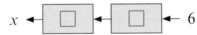

$x \leftarrow \boxed{\square} \leftarrow \boxed{\square} \leftarrow 6$

b   Use the reverse function machine to solve the equation $\frac{x}{4} - 5 = 6$.

8 Follow the instructions for each equation.

i   Draw a function machine.

ii   Draw the reverse function machine.

iii   Use the reverse function machine to solve the equation.

a $x + 11 = 37$ b $k - 17 = 6$ c $3t = 36$

d $4x + 12 = 20$ e $3n - 14 = 22$ f $5(y - 7) = 45$

g $3(q + 10) = 39$ h $2t + 9 = 20$ i $2(m - 8) = 3$

j $\frac{a}{3} - 9 = 5$ k $\frac{r}{10} + 1 = 16$ l $\frac{k - 12}{7} = 10$

Angles

- Recognising and naming different types of angle
- Measuring angles
- Calculating angles

Keywords

You should know

explanation 1

1 Describe each of these angles. The first one has been done for you.

a

Acute

b

c

d

e

f

g

h

i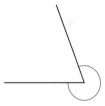

explanation 2a   explanation 2b

2 Sophie is measuring an *acute* angle between two lines with a 180° protractor.

The diagram shows part of the protractor scale and one of the lines.

Read the scale to find the size of the angle.

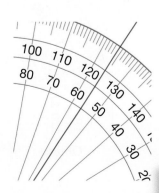

3 Find the *acute* angles shown on these protractor scales.

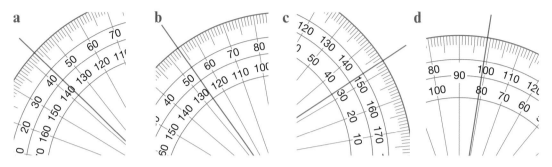

a   b   c   d

4 Find the *obtuse* angles shown on these protractor scales.

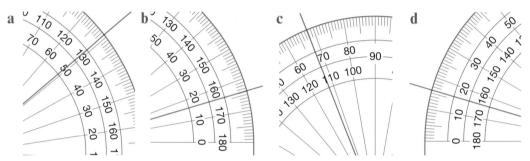

a   b   c   d

5 Jeremy is measuring a *reflex* angle between two lines with a 360° protractor.

The diagram shows part of the protractor scale and one of the lines.

Read the scale to find the size of the angle.

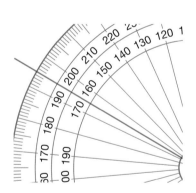

6 Use the information given on these diagrams to find the unknown angles.

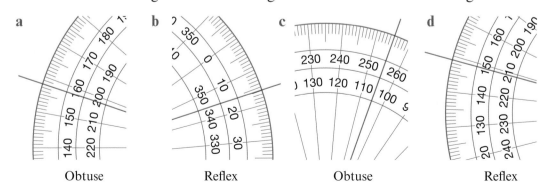

a   b   c   d

Obtuse   Reflex   Obtuse   Reflex

7 Measure these angles with a protractor.

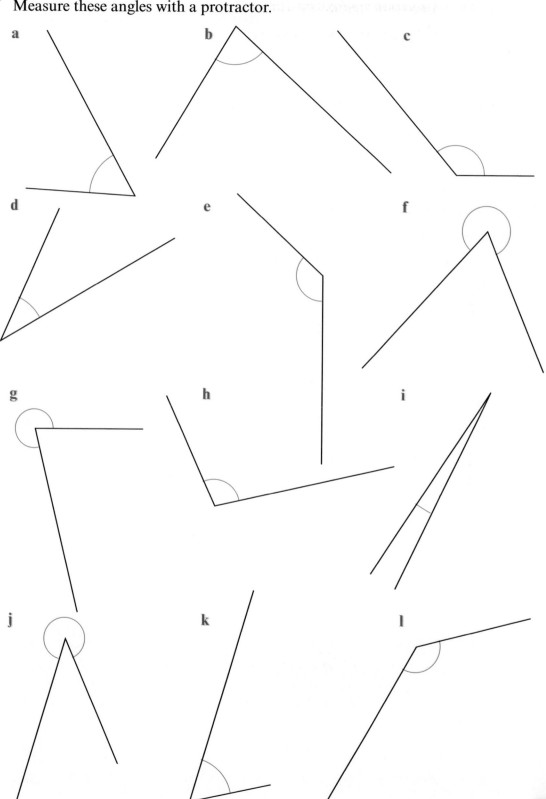

8 Here are some angles marked with letters.

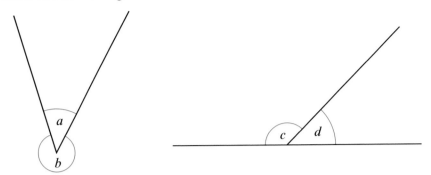

What can you say about the value of *a* + *b*?

What can you say about the value of *c* + *d*?

explanation 3a   explanation 3b   explanation 3c

9 Work out the size of each angle marked with a letter.

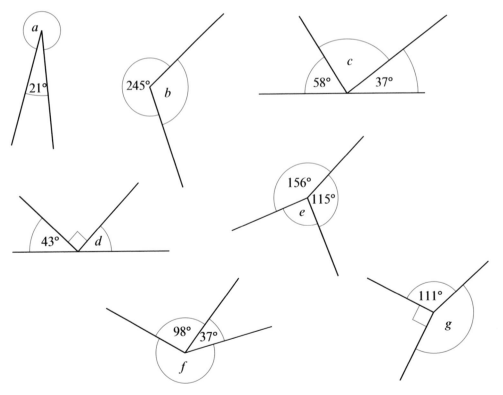

explanation 4

10 Work out the size of each angle marked with a letter.

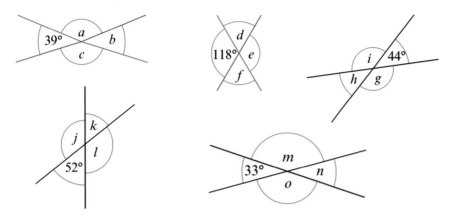

explanation 5

11 Work out the angles marked with letters.

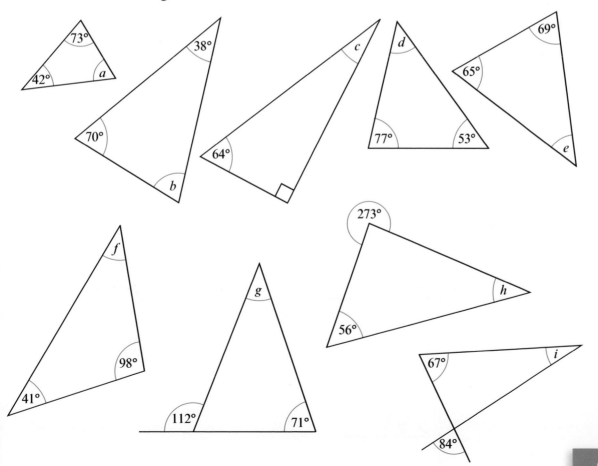

explanation 6

12 Work out the angles marked with letters.

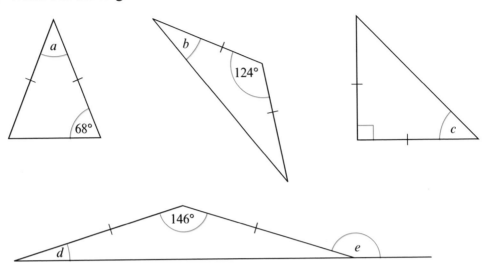

13 Work out the angles marked with letters.

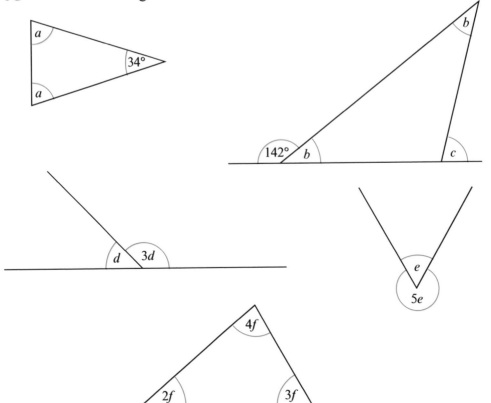

14 The Earth makes one full turn on its axis every
24 hours.

    a What angle does the Earth turn through in
8 hours?

    b How long does it take for the Earth to turn
through a right angle?

15 How high is the tree?
Explain how you know.

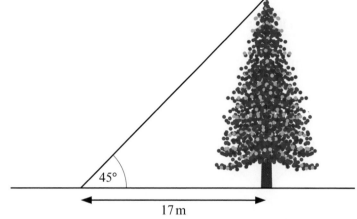

45°

17 m

16 a Through what angle does the minute hand of
a clock turn in 30 minutes?

    b Through what angle does the hour hand of a
clock turn in 30 minutes?

    c What is the obtuse angle between the minute
hand and hour hand of a clock at 12:30?

17 Find the value of x and the perimeter of the triangle.
Explain how you obtained your answers.

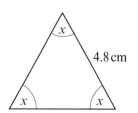

x

4.8 cm

x x

Lines, shapes and coordinates

- Investigating properties of parallel lines
- Recognising and naming different types of quadrilateral
- Recognising line symmetry
- Plotting coordinates in 4 quadrants

Keywords

You should know

explanation 1a   explanation 1b

1 List all of the lines in the diagram that are

   a parallel to AB   **b** parallel to CD   **c** perpendicular to CD

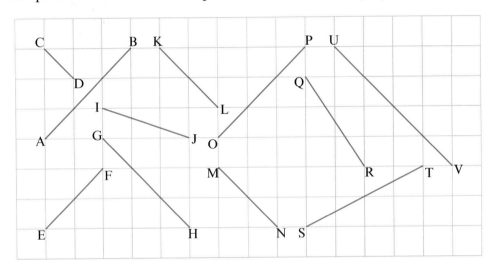

2 Measure the distance between this pair of parallel lines to the nearest 0.1 cm.

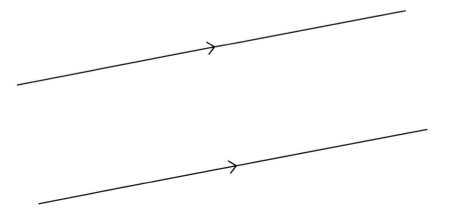

3 a AB, CD and EF are line segments.

- AB is parallel to CD
- CD is parallel to EF

What can you say about AB and EF?

b J, K and L are points. If JK is parallel to KL, what can you say about J, K and L?

explanation 2

4 The diagram shows three partly completed quadrilaterals. ABCD is a parallelogram, PQRS is a kite and WXYZ is a trapezium. Copy and complete the diagrams.

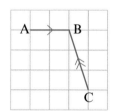 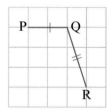 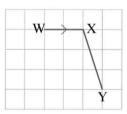

explanation 3

5 Copy and complete each diagram so that the dotted line is a line of symmetry.

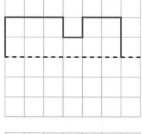 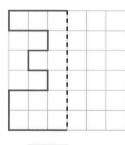 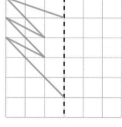

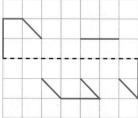 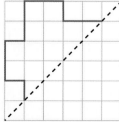 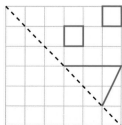

6 Copy these diagrams and draw any lines of symmetry.
Write down the name of each shape.

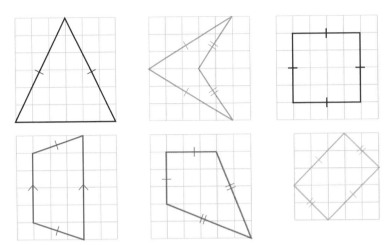

7 a Draw a triangle with 3 lines of symmetry. What is this triangle's special name?

b Draw a trapezium with no lines of symmetry.

c How many lines of symmetry can a parallelogram have?

d How many lines of symmetry does a rhombus have?

e Draw a right-angled isosceles triangle. Draw any lines of symmetry.

f Is it possible to draw a triangle with exactly 2 lines of symmetry? Explain your answer.

explanation 4a   explanation 4b

8 Write down the coordinates of each of the labelled points.

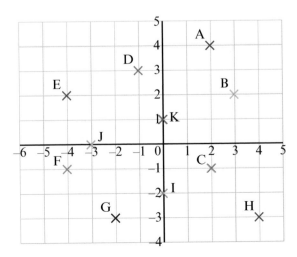

9 a Plot the points P(0, 5), Q(6, 6), R(8, 1), S(2, 0) and join them in order with straight lines.

b Write down the coordinates of the mid-point of

   i P and R   **ii** Q and S

c What do you notice about your answers to part **b**?

d Draw the diagonals of PQRS. What do you notice about the point where they cross?

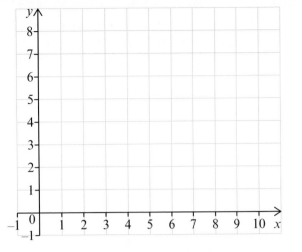

10 Draw x- and y-axes labelled from −6 to 6.

  a Plot the following points and join them in order with straight lines.

    (−4, −5) (4, 3) (−4, 3) (0, 6) (4, 3) (4, −5) (−4, −5) (−4, 3) (4, −5)

  b How many lines of symmetry does the shape have?

  c How many pairs of parallel sides are there?

  d How many triangles does the shape contain?

  e How many of the triangles are right angled?

  f What are the coordinates of the point where the diagonals of the square cross?

11 Draw x- and y-axes labelled from −6 to 6.

  a Plot the points (1, 1) (−1, −1) and (−1, 1)

  b What are the coordinates of a fourth point that would make a square?

  c What are the coordinates of a fourth point that would make a parallelogram?

  d What are the coordinates of a fourth point that would make a kite?

  e What are the coordinates of a fourth point that would make an arrowhead?

12 Calculate the area of each of the possible shapes found in question **11**.

Surveys and experiments

- Planning and conducting a survey
- Conducting a mathematical experiment
- Using an appropriate type of data for a given purpose

Keywords

You should know

explanation 1

Youth crime figures soar in village
Parents blame lack of resources
Nothing to do

One suggestion put forward in response to the newspaper article was to start a new youth club in the area. A group of villagers held a meeting to discuss the idea and this raised some questions.

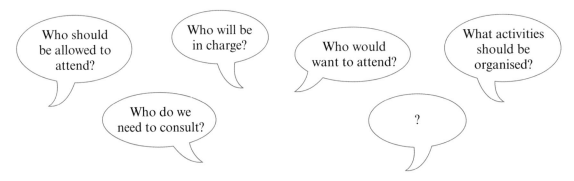

Who should be allowed to attend?

Who will be in charge?

Who would want to attend?

What activities should be organised?

Who do we need to consult?

?

1 Discuss these questions in a group. Write down some more questions that should be considered.

2 Make a list of groups of people that should be consulted in a survey. Write down some questions that you might ask each group.

explanation 2

3 Take a look at these questions. Say why each one would not be suitable for a survey in its present form.

   a Most people want more car parking space available in the town. Do you agree?

   b How much do you earn?

   c How old are you?

   d Are you in favour of making animals suffer for medical research?

   e What are your views on the state of the economy?

   f What do you think about young people?

   g What qualifications do you have?

   h Why do you think women make better drivers than men?

   i How could recycling be made more effective?

4 The question is often clearer if you offer choices.

Instead of simply asking for a person's age, for example, you could ask them to select an age-range:

> Offering choices may also make the question easier to answer, while providing you with enough information.

Less than 18 ☐

18 to 25 ☐

Over 25 ☐

Write some suitable choices for each of these questions.

   a How much time do you spend each day watching television?

   b Approximately how many times have you visited a cinema in the last year?

   c Do you think computers have helped to raise standards in education?

   d How many miles do you travel by car in a typical year?

   e Do you think that calculators should be used in primary schools?

5 The following question is politely phrased and offers choices, but there is still something wrong. What is the problem?

How many times per week do you eat meat?

Once   Twice   Three times or more

6 Explain why it wouldn't be easy to write suitable choices for the following question.

What is your favourite holiday resort?

---

explanation 3

---

7 Look back at the questions that you wrote for the youth club survey in question **1**.

   a   Try to improve your questions and add some new ones.

   b   Design a data collection sheet for your questions.

   c   Test your data collection sheet with a small group of people.
       Make any changes needed to improve it.

8 Carry out a survey using either your youth club data collection sheet or a new data collection sheet based on a different enquiry.

Make sure that the data collected represents the situation fairly.

Remember that the day, time and location all affect who is available to answer your questions.

Use a variety of charts to present your data.

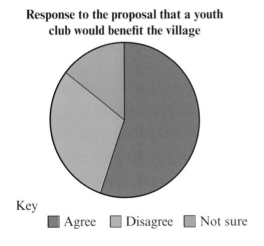

Response to the proposal that a youth club would benefit the village

Key
■ Agree   ■ Disagree   ■ Not sure

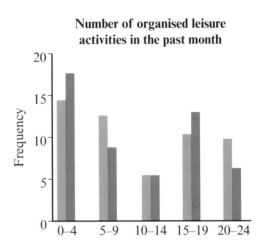

Number of organised leisure activities in the past month

Make some statements about what your survey shows.

Treat all of the information fairly – even if you disagree with it!

Try to draw some conclusions that will help to develop your project.

explanation 4

9 a Cut a piece of card in the shape of a square of
side 4 cm.
Draw the diagonals of the square and label its
sides from 1 to 4.
Push a cocktail stick through the centre to make
a spinner.

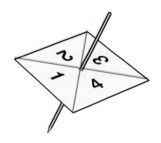

b In an experiment, the spinner is spun and the results are recorded.
If you carry out lots of trials, what would you expect to happen to the
frequency of each possible score?

c Copy this table.
Carry out 40 trials and
record your results in
the table.
Comment on your
results. Are they what
you expected?

Score	Tally	Frequency
1		
2		
3		
4		

d Move the cocktail stick about 0.8 cm from the
centre along the diagonal between 1 and 2.
Describe how you think this might affect the
results.
Do you think the direction of spin will make a
difference?

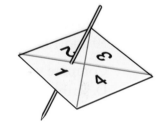

e Carry out 40 trials, spinning clockwise each time.
Record your results in a table. Comment on your results.

f Carry out another 40 trials, spinning anticlockwise each time.
Record your results in a table.
Does the direction of spin appear to make a difference?
Compare your results with others in the class.

10 Decide whether you would use primary data, secondary data or experimental
data to investigate the following questions.

a Do more people visit the cinema regularly now than 10 years ago?

b Do people feel that traffic speed cameras make the roads safer?

c Is the population of the country increasing or decreasing?

d Is a piece of toast more likely to land jam side down?

Experiments and probability

- Exploring the results of a large number of trials
- Using coins and dice to produce random outcomes
- Estimating a probability

explanation 1

1 a In an experiment, a coin is flipped repeatedly and the results recorded.
Write down the expected number of heads and tails from these trials.

   i   10 trials   ii   50 trials   iii   100 trials

b Copy the table. Work
with a partner to carry
out the experiment
described in part a.

	Heads	Tails
10 trials		
50 trials		
100 trials		

c Write the percentage of
heads and tails after 10,
50 and 100 trials.

d Compare your percentage results with others in the class.
Describe how the results for 100 trials are different from the results for 10 trials.

explanation 2

2 Ali has a large bag of balls. She picks one at random,
looks at the colour and puts it back in the bag.
She does this 50 times. This table shows Ali's results.

Red	Blue	Yellow
19	23	8

Use the table to estimate the probability that the ball selected at random will be

a red   b blue   c yellow

3 In a survey of 400 customers at a supermarket, 24 prefer full-fat milk, 296 prefer
semi-skimmed milk, and 76 prefer skimmed milk. the remainder don't drink milk.

Estimate the probability that a customer selected at random

a prefers semi-skimmed milk   b prefers skimmed milk

c prefers full-fat milk   d doesn't drink milk

4 Heads I win!

This is a game for two players.

Blue wins					●					Red wins

How to play

You need a coin and a counter.

Copy the game board making each square large enough for your counter. Put the counter in the middle.

Take turns to flip the coin. First player is the red player.

Whenever red plays, heads moves the counter one square right and tails moves it left.

Whenever blue plays, heads moves the counter one square left and tails moves it right.

Play continues until one player wins.

Before you start ...

a   Is one player more likely to win than the other?

b   What is the smallest number of flips of the coin needed to find a winner?

c   Do you think it is very likely that a game will be won with the smallest number of flips?

Play the game several times

Keep a tally of the number of times the coin is flipped in each game.

d   What is the largest number of flips needed to complete one of your games? Compare your results with others in the class.

e   Estimate the probability that a game will be won with the smallest number of flips.

f   Estimate the probability that at least 20 turns are needed to complete a game.

g   Change the rules of the game to give one player an advantage. Play the game several times.

Does the player with the advantage always win?

Mental methods

- Organising a calculation so that you can work it out mentally

Keywords

You should know

explanation 1

1 Copy the diagrams. Fill in the missing values to show the calculations.

    a 48 + 23   **b** 129 + 64

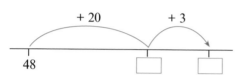
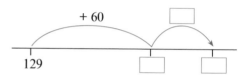

    c 56 + 49   **d** 247 + 78

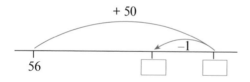
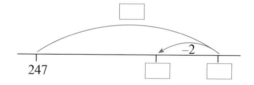

2 Work out.

    a 37 + 54   **b** 65 + 38   **c** 136 + 57

    d 426 + 69   **e** 317 + 44   **f** 428 + 239

    g 278 + 188   **h** 337 + 453   **i** 112 + 344

3 Copy these diagrams and fill in the missing values to show the calculations.

    a 220 − 63   **b** 473 − 149

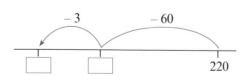
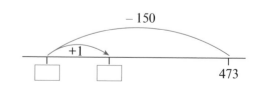

4 Work out these differences.

    a 170 − 51   **b** 318 − 64   **c** 143 − 49

    d 261 − 178   **e** 625 − 219   **f** 732 − 516

    g 817 − 472   **h** 227 − 169   **i** 563 − 418

5 Copy and complete.

    a $37 + \square = 100$ **b** $453 + \square = 1000$ **c** $8.9 + \square = 10$

    d $4.36 + \square = 10$ **e** $87.4 + \square = 100$ **f** $41.8 + \square = 100$

    g $£7.80 + \square = £10$ **h** $£4.68 + \square = £10$ **i** $£34.80 + \square = £100$

6 Work these out.

    a 100 − 68   **b** 10 − 4.1   **c** 10 − 3.65

    d 100 − 9.27   **e** 100 − 57.9   **f** 100 − 19.38

    g 100 − 26.4   **h** 100 − 89.21   **i** 10 − 0.78

7 Find the change given from a £10 note for each of these costs.

    a £9.70   **b** £6.40   **c** £3.32   **d** £4.47   **e** £1.96   **f** 58p

8 Copy and complete. Each number in a rectangle is the sum of the numbers in the circles on either side.

    a

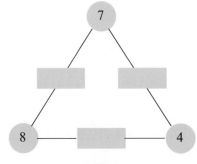

    b

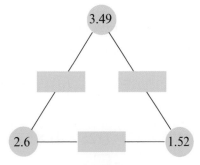

    c

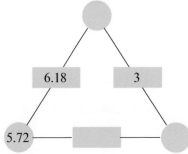

    d

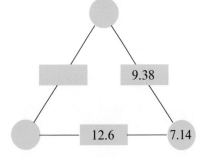

9 These calculations show some different ways to partition a multiplication. Copy and complete.

a $43 \times 6 = (40 \times 6) + (\square \times 6)$

$= \square + \square$

$= \square$

b $39 \times 7 = (40 \times 7) - (\square \times 7)$

$= \square - \square$

$= \square$

c $3.7 \times 11 = (3.7 \times 10) + (3.7 \times \square)$

$= \square + \square$

$= \square$

d $5.8 \times 9 = (5.8 \times 10) - (5.8 \times \square)$

$= \square - \square$

$= \square$

10 Use partitioning to work out these multiplications mentally.

a 23×8 **b** 99×7 **c** 6×54

d 72×11 **e** 198×3 **f** 81×99

11 Use partitioning to work out these multiplications mentally.

a 6.8×11 **b** 12.9×3 **c** 5.7×9

d 10.1×36 **e** 48×9.9 **f** 12×38

12 Copy and complete.

a $25 \times 36 = (25 \times 4) \times \square$

$= \square \times \square$

$= \square$

b $2.5 \times 24 = (2.5 \times 4) \times \square$

$= \square \times \square$

$= \square$

c $125 \times 12 = (125 \times 4) \times \square$

$= \square \times \square$

$= \square$

d $12.5 \times 16 = (12.5 \times 2) \times \square$

$= \square \times \square$

$= \square$

e $6.4 \times 30 = (6.4 \times 10) \times \square$

$= \square \times \square$

$= \square$

f $0.92 \times 400 = (0.92 \times 100) \times \square$

$= \square \times \square$

$= \square$

13 Work these out.

a 25×16 b 25×17 c 25×14

d 125×8 e 125×9 f 125×32

g 2.5×12 h 7.5×12 i 1.25×24

j 3.2×40 k 0.72×300 l 0.75×400

> Look for connections between the questions that may help you work out the answers.

14 Copy and complete.

a $4.86 \times 50 = \square \times 100$
$ = \square$

b $12.5 \times 14 = 25 \times \square$
$ = \square$

c £7.50 $\times 60 = £15 \times \square$
$ = \square$

d £6.25 $\times 44 = £25 \times \square$
$ = \square$

15 George works 5 days per week. He saves £7.50 each day by walking to work instead of driving. How much will George save after these times?

a 1 week b 4 weeks c 50 weeks

16 Work these out.

a 4.5×8 b 11.5×12 c £2.25 $\times 16$

d £32 $\times 1.25$ e £96 $\times 1.125$ f $96 \times £7.50$

g £28 $\times 2.5$ h $1.625 \times £32$ i £1.25 $\times 84$

17 Zeynep swam 48 lengths of a swimming pool to raise money for charity. How much did she raise if she is sponsored these amounts per length?

a £1.50 b £3.25 c £4.25

 explanation 4

*__18__ $139 \times 48 = 6672$. Use this fact to work out these.

a 139×24 b 139×480 c 139×16

d 1.39×48 e 13.9×0.48 f 13.9×24

19 Each calculation is equal to 2.75×400. What are the missing numbers?

a $275 \times \square$ b $5.5 \times \square$ c $11 \times \square$

20 24 × 136 = 3264. Use this fact to work out these.

    a 3264 ÷ 24   **b** 3264 ÷ 136   **c** 3264 ÷ 48

    d 3264 ÷ 12   **e** 3264 ÷ 68   **f** 6528 ÷ 272

---

explanation 5

21 a Which of these numbers are divisible by 3?

        1467   2513   8215   7324   6543   5437

   b Are any of the numbers divisible by 6? Explain your answer.

22 Write a 6-digit number divisible by 30.

23 Only one of the numbers below is divisible by 15.

    42368 76542 97650 86735 65874 98124 31576

   a Describe an efficient way to find the number.

   b Which number is it?

24 Write a 5-digit number which is divisible by

    a 9   **b** 18   **c** 45   **d** 18 and 45

---

explanation 6

25 Copy and complete these calculations.

   a $1200 \div 24 = \dfrac{1200}{24}$ **b** $134 \div 50 = \dfrac{\square}{50}$

                   $= \dfrac{100}{\square}$ $= \dfrac{\square}{100}$

                   $= \square$ $= \square$

26 Work these out.

    a 432 ÷ 18   **b** 8250 ÷ 150   **c** 6300 ÷ 450

27 Work these out.

    a 423 ÷ 50   **b** 321 ÷ 25   **c** 216 ÷ 75

Written methods for multiplying and dividing

- Multiplying and dividing using written methods
- Estimating the value of calculations

Keywords

You should know

explanation 1a   explanation 1b

1 Work these out. Show your method.

    a 24×6 **b** 32×5 **c** 41×8 **d** 362×4 **e** 507×9 **f** 856×7

2 Use $423 \times 9 = 3807$ to calculate these.

    a 42.3×9 **b** 4.23×9 **c** 8.46×9

3 a Work these out.

    i 576×4 **ii** 812×6 **iii** 284×5

  b Use your answers to part **a** to write the answer to each calculation.

    i 5.76×4 **ii** 57.6×4 **iii** 81.2×6

    iv 28.4×5 **v** 8.12×6 **vi** 2.84×5

4 Work these out.

    a 3.6×4 **b** 7.3×8 **c** 0.26×3

    d 0.71×5 **e** 5.2×5 **f** 0.59×9

explanation 2

3429   1729   5144   4404

5 a Which answer belongs with which calculation? Use estimation to find out.

    i 643×8 **ii** 247×7 **iii** 381×9 **iv** 734×6

  b Write the value of each calculation.

    i 24.7×7 **ii** 6.43×8 **iii** 73.4×6 **iv** 3.81×9

  c Work out the value of $64.3 \times 8 + 6 \times 7.34$.

6 Work these out.

a 2.43×5 b 82.4×6 c 9×1.72

d 3.65×4 e $11 + 7 \times 5.32$ f $8(1.34 + 7.6)$

7 Work these out.

a   £9.27 × 5   b   £1.76 × 4   c   9 × £8.32

8 Socks cost £2.48 per pair and t-shirts cost £9.94 each. Jennie buys six pairs of socks and three t-shirts. The shopkeeper says the total cost is £54.70.

a   Use estimation to show that £54.70 is too much.

b   Work out how much Jennie should pay.

9 Glasses cost £7.95 each. Steve has a £50 note. He wants to buy 6 glasses.

a   Use estimation to show that Steve has enough money.

b   Work out how much change Steve will receive.

10 The diagram shows one view of a machine part. The labelled lengths were originally measured accurately in inches.

A new part is to be made of the same size but converted to cm using 1" = 2.54 cm.

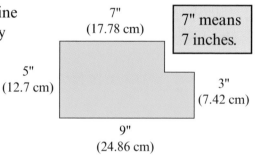

a   Find out which measurements have not been converted correctly.

b   Work out the correct values.

explanation 3a   explanation 3b

11 Work these out.

a 24×16 b 34×53 c 28×65

d 21×86 e 82×94 f 76×43

12 Work these out.

a 247×31 b 546×44 c 63×128

13 Sundeep earns £376 per week. How much will he earn in a year?

explanation 4a explanation 4b

14 Write an estimate for each division and then find the exact value.

a $576 \div 6$ b $315 \div 7$ c $520 \div 5$

d $5247 \div 3$ e $3456 \div 9$ f $17\,864 \div 8$

15 Work these out.

a $12.6 \div 3$ b $7.24 \div 4$ c $39.2 \div 8$

d $524.4 \div 6$ e $89.45 \div 5$ f $2483.6 \div 7$

16 Eight ice creams cost £7.76.
Were they more, or less, than £1 each?
Work out the price of each ice cream.

17 Five friends share the total cost of £147 for a meal at a restaurant.
How much do they each have to pay?

18 Calculate the mean of 4.63, 7.25, 6.78 and 5.3.

19 Write an estimate for each division and then find the exact value.

a $575 \div 23$ b $868 \div 31$ c $748 \div 17$

20 Copy and complete. The numbers in the rectangles are the product of the numbers in the circles on either side.

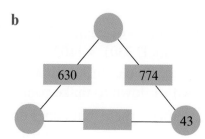

21 A kitchen floor measures 551 cm by 483 cm. It is to be covered with floor tiles.
The tiles measure 29 cm by 23 cm.
How many tiles are needed?

Using a calculator (2)

- Using the = key to change the order of operations
- Using inverse operations to check a calculation
- Using a calculator to find remainders after division
- Using remainders when solving problems

Keywords

You should know

explanation 1a   explanation 1b

1 Copy the crossword puzzle.

Each clue has a calculation that should help you.

Once you have a calculator answer, look at the display upside down and compare it with the clue. Write the word in the space.

To read your upside-down display:

$1 \rightarrow I, 2 \rightarrow C, 3 \rightarrow E, 5 \rightarrow S$

$6 \rightarrow G, 7 \rightarrow L, 8 \rightarrow B, 0 \rightarrow O$ or D

Across

1 Reveals the hidden meaning $40\,771 \times 130$

6 Poem $20^2 - 10^2$

7 Not hot $\dfrac{25^2 + 77}{1000}$

8 Compass direction $\sqrt{1225}$

9 You might find this on a door $2 \times 53 \times 73$

13 Combines to mean earth $\left(\frac{3}{5}\right)^2$

14 A cube has twelve of these $11^2 \times 443$

Down

1 Used in games of chance $30(9^2 + 2(2^2 + 3^2))$

2 After school? 3301×1102

3 One more than even $1 \div 1000$ to 2 d.p.

4 Mix with 1 down to make your mind up $\sqrt{(5 \times 180)}$

5 Squares have these, but cubes don't $5 \times \sqrt{529} \times (21^2 + 20)$

10 The ones who followed $\dfrac{2.4^2 + 0.4^2}{16}$

11 Not just a stick $\dfrac{4766}{16} + \dfrac{2473}{8}$

12 Measure of capacity $\sqrt{54} \times \sqrt{96}$

2 Undo these calculations to find the missing values.

a $\square \div 9 = 8.76$ b $\square + 173.89 = 312.6$ c $\square \times 1.175 = 28.905$

d $\sqrt{\square} = 16.2$ e $\square - 97.34 = 421.8$ f $(\square)^2 = 69.8896$

3 I have the answer 102.1348 and I multiplied 12.395 by something to obtain it.

What did I multiply by?

4 **a** Keira obtained the answer shown on her calculator. The number represents an amount shown in pounds. What should Keira write down as her answer?

b Use a calculator to work these out and write your answers in pounds.

　i £1786.37 − £948.87   **ii** £78.37 + £198.32 + £217.51

　iii 86p × 45   **iv** (£973 + £279) ÷ 5

c Undo these calculations to find the missing values.

　i $\square \div 12 = £17.45$ **ii** $\square \times 9.6 = £313.92$

5 Work these out. Check your answers by using inverse operations.

a $113.687 \div 14.9$ b 9.81×15.6 c 8.743^2

d $\sqrt{41.6025}$ e 2.3×7.8^2 f $5.9 \times \sqrt{73.96}$

6 Find the remainder for each of these divisions.

a $546 \div 17$ b $2310 \div 9$ c $824 \div 31$

d $2562 \div 68$ e $9751 \div 53$ f $6214 \div 39$

7 5000 nails are put into a machine. The machine puts them into packs that contain 27 nails each.

   a How many packs of nails can be made?

   b How many nails are left over?

8 a How many company shares costing £11.24 each can be bought with £400?

   b How much change will be given?

9 A school day trip is organised for 548 pupils. All of the pupils travel on coaches that can carry 47 pupils each.

   a How many coaches are needed?

   b Calculate the number of empty seats.

explanation 4 ──

10 Calculate these to the nearest penny.

   a £18.32 × 3.6   b £34.79 × 2.3   c £761 ÷ 12

   d £46.10 ÷ 3   e 4.8 × (£7.26 + £1.73)   f (£17.32 − £4.78) ÷ 7

11 You can add VAT to an amount by multiplying it by 1.175.
   Add VAT to the following amounts and give each answer to the nearest penny.

   a £19.50   b £67.89   c £2376.30

   d £764.83   e £5177   f £8723.50

12 Calculate the area of each these shapes to the nearest $0.1\,\text{m}^2$.

   a

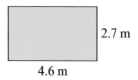

   2.7 m

   4.6 m

   b

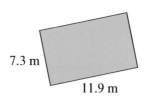

   7.3 m

   11.9 m

   c

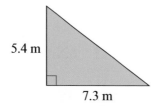

   5.4 m

   7.3 m

   d

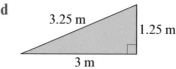

   3.25 m

   1.25 m

   3 m

Expressions and equations

- Simplifying algebraic expressions
- Solving equations using inverse operations
- Expanding brackets

Keywords

You should know

explanation 1a   explanation 1b

1 Write an expression for each set of instructions.
Start with x.

 a Multiply by 4.

 b Subtract 6.

 c Add 14.

 d Divide by 3.

 e Subtract from 5.

2 Write an expression for each set of instructions.
Start with x.

 a Subtract 11 then divide the answer by 5.

 b Add 7 then multiply the answer by 2.

 c Multiply by 3 then add 5 and divide the answer by 4.

 d Subtract from 10 and multiply the answer by 3.

 e Divide by 3 then add 5.

3 Write an expression for each set of instructions.
Start with y.

 a Divide by 10.

 b Multiply by 3 and divide by 5.

 c Divide by 4 then subtract 3.

 d Multiply by 5 then subtract the answer from 17.

 e Subtract 9 and divide 20 by the answer.

 f Multiply by 3 then divide by 4 and subtract the answer from 10.

4 Write the instructions contained in these expressions. Start with x.

    a $2(x - 5)$ **b** $21 - 5x$ **c** $\frac{x}{3} + 4$

    d $\frac{x + 8}{4}$ **e** $35 - 4(x + 1)$ **f** $\frac{18}{x - 3}$

5 Find the value of each of these expressions when $x = 5$.

    a $3(x + 2)$ **b** $11 + 2x$ **c** $\frac{4x - 2}{3}$

    d $\frac{35}{x}$ **e** $10 + 3(x + 1)$ **f** $x(x - 2)$

    g $x(x + 1)$ **h** $\frac{x + 10}{x}$ **i** $2x - \frac{3x}{5}$

6 Give the value of these expressions as mixed numbers when $x = 9$.

    a $\frac{x}{4}$ **b** $\frac{2x}{5}$ **c** $\frac{x + 1}{3}$ **d** $\frac{10}{x}$ **e** $3 + \frac{x}{4}$ **f** $x - \frac{x}{5}$

> **explanation 2**

7 Simplify each of these expressions.

    a $2x - 3 + 3$ **b** $\frac{x}{4} + 7 - 7$ **c** $\frac{5x}{5}$

    d $\frac{3x}{3}$ **e** $\frac{x}{4} \times 4$ **f** $\frac{x + 3}{7} \times 7$

8 Copy and complete the following expressions so that they simplify to x.

    a $x + 8 - \square$ **b** $x - 9 + \square$ **c** $x - \square + 6$

    d $\frac{4x}{\square}$ **e** $\frac{4x}{\square} + 5 - \square$ **f** $\frac{x - 9}{7} \times \square + \square$

9 Copy and complete these function machines.

    a $2x + 3 \rightarrow \boxed{-3} \xrightarrow{2x} \boxed{\square} \rightarrow x$ **b** $3x - 5 \rightarrow \boxed{\square} \xrightarrow{\square} \boxed{\square} \rightarrow x$

    c $\frac{x + 7}{4} \rightarrow \boxed{\square} \xrightarrow{\square} \boxed{\square} \rightarrow x$ **d** $\frac{x}{5} - 6 \rightarrow \boxed{\square} \xrightarrow{\square} \boxed{\square} \rightarrow x$

    e $3(x + 2) \rightarrow \boxed{\square} \xrightarrow{\square} \boxed{\square} \rightarrow x$ **f** $\frac{4x}{5} \rightarrow \boxed{\square} \xrightarrow{\square} \boxed{\square} \rightarrow x$

explanation 3

10 Copy and complete.

a $5x = 45$

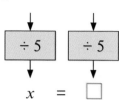

$x = \square$

b $4x + 11 = 39$

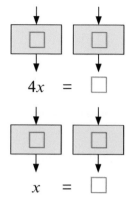

$4x = \square$

$x = \square$

c $\frac{x}{3} - 7 = 118$

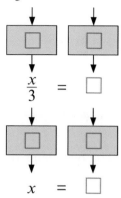

$\frac{x}{3} = \square$

$x = \square$

11 Solve these equations.

a $\frac{x}{10} = 17$

b $4x = 64$

c $x + 99 = 147$

d $x - 134 = 270$

e $\frac{x}{11} = 20$

f $12x = 60$

12 Solve these equations.

a $x - 47 = 86$

b $10x = 140$

c $5x = 75$

d $\frac{x}{8} = 31$

e $x + 58 = 94$

f $\frac{x}{25} = 4$

13 Copy and complete the steps to solve the following equations.

a $3x - 17 = 16$

$3x = \square$

$x = \square$

b $2(x + 12) = 68$

$x + 12 = \square$

$x = \square$

c $\frac{x}{5} + 112 = 126$

$\frac{x}{5} = \square$

$x = \square$

d $\frac{5x}{3} = 15$

$5x = \square$

$x = \square$

e $11 = \frac{x - 19}{6}$

$\square = x - 19$

$x = \square$

f $75 = 5(x - 32)$

$\square = x - 32$

$x = \square$

g $2 = \frac{x + 10}{4}$

$\square = x + 10$

$x = \square$

h $9 = 3(4 - x)$

$\square = 4 - x$

$x = \square$

i $x = \frac{x + 4}{2}$

$\square = x + 4$

$x = \square$

14   Solve these equations.

a $\dfrac{x - 24}{8} = 7$

b $9x + 73 = 109$

c $11(x + 14) = 220$

d $17 = \dfrac{x}{4} - 53$

e $25 = \dfrac{x + 81}{4}$

f $40 = \dfrac{8x}{3}$

*15   Solve these equations and give your answers as fractions in their simplest form.

a $10x = 5$

b $12x = 8$

c $25x = 15$

d $12x + 10 = 19$

e $25x - 9 = 11$

f $24 = 18x + 12$

explanation 4 ────────────────────────────────

16   The perimeter of the rectangle shown is 76 cm.

a   Write this information as an equation and simplify it.

b   Solve the equation.

c   Find the length of the longest side of the rectangle.

17 cm

3x cm

17   a   Write an equation involving the sum of the angles of this triangle and simplify it.

b   Solve the equation.

c   Find the angles of the triangle.

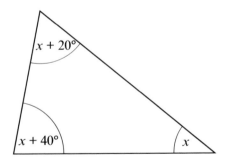

$x + 20°$

$x + 40°$

x

18   In the diagram, AB is a straight line.

a   Write an equation involving the sum of the angles shown and simplify it.

b   Solve the equation.

c   Write down the size of each of the labelled angles.

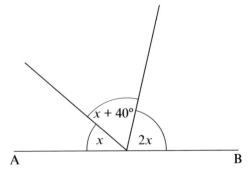

$x + 40°$

x $2x$

A

B

explanation 5

19 Do you think that the statement $x + y = y + x$ is always true, sometimes true or never true for numbers x and y? Give two examples to support your answer.

20 Repeat question **19** for each of the following statements.

a $x - y = y - x$

b $x - y = -(y - x)$

c $xy = yx$

d $\dfrac{x}{y} = \dfrac{y}{x}$

e $x + y + 1 = -(1 - y - x)$

f $(1 - x) - (1 + y) = -(x + y)$

explanation 6

21 Simplify each of these expressions.

a $xy + 2yx$

b $5zx + xz$

c $2xy + 3yx - xy$

d $5pq - 3qp$

e $rp + 6pr - 2$

f $pq + qp + pr$

g $a \times b \times c$

h $2 \times w \times 3$

i $2pq + q \times 6 \times p$

22 a Work out these multiplications.

i $(5 \times 4) \times 3$ ii $5 \times (4 \times 3)$ iii $(3 \times 8) \times 2$ iv $3 \times (8 \times 2)$

v $(7 \times 3) \times 5$ vi $7 \times (3 \times 5)$ vii $(4 \times 11) \times 2$ viii $4 \times (11 \times 2)$

b Copy and complete. $(xy)z = \square$

23 Write down which of the following expressions always have the same value as xyz.

zxy $x(yz)$ yxz $y(zx)$

24 Find the value of xyz when

a $x = 3, y = 5, z = 20$

b $x = 4, y = 25, z = 9$

c $x = 2, y = 2.5, z = 7$

d $x = 10, y = 2, z = 1.9$

e $x = \dfrac{1}{2}, y = 12, z = 11$

f $x = \dfrac{1}{2}, y = 7.9, z = 20$

> Choose the simplest order to work out each calculation.

25 Simplify the following expressions.

a $3pqr + 2rpq$

b $p(qr) + 6rpq$

c $10r(qp) - pqr$

d $4pqr + 11r(qp) - prq$

26 Simplify these expressions. The first one is done for you.

   a $2 \times 4p = (2 \times 4)p = 8p$ **b** $3 \times 5q$ **c** $4 \times 7t$

   d $8r \times 3$ **e** $9n \times 4$ **f** $10k \times 3$

27 Simplify these expressions. The first one is done for you.

   a $4 \times 3g + 5 \times 2g = 12g + 10g$ **b** $3 \times 4w + 2 \times 7w$
                              $= 22g$

   c $5 \times 4v - 3 \times 3v$ **d** $7 \times 3x - 5x \times 4$

   e $6 \times 4y + y - 3 \times 2y$ **f** $a + 3a \times 5 - 2 \times 4a$

*28 Find and simplify an expression for the area of each of these figures.

a
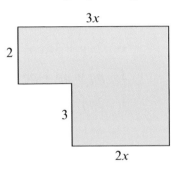

b
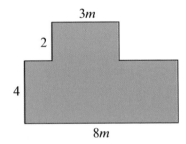

c
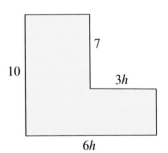

d
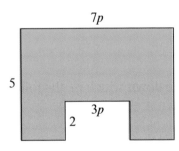

e
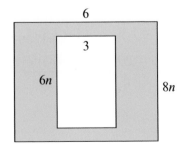

f
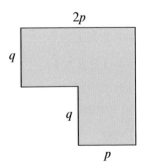

*29 Copy and complete the statement to show the total area in two different ways.

$5(x + \square) = 5x + \square$

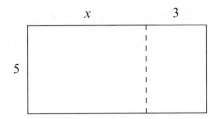

*30 Copy and complete the statement to show the coloured area in two different ways.

$3(y - \square) = \square - 12$

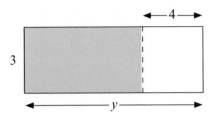

explanation 7

31 Copy and complete the following steps to work out 24×19.

$$24 \times 19 = 24\,(20 - \square)$$
$$= 24 \times \square - 24 \times \square$$
$$= \square - \square$$
$$= \square$$

32 Use the method shown in question **31** to work out these calculations.

a 32×29 b 14×49 c 18×9.9

33 Expand the brackets in these expressions.

a $4(x + 5)$ b $6(n - 4)$ c $3(5 + t)$

d $10(12 - h)$ e $8(7 + p)$ f $9(11 - b)$

g $x(3 + y)$ h $r(5 - t)$ i $k(n + 2)$

34 Expand the brackets in these expressions.

a $3(2x + 1)$ b $4(3n - 2)$ c $5(4 - 2k)$

d $6(10 + 3j)$ e $2(9 - 5e)$ f $7(3d + 4)$

g $a(2b + 5)$ h $g(9 - 3t)$ i $2z(5 + 3y)$

*35 Use the diagram to help you complete the statement below.

$4(x + \square + \square) = \boxed{}$

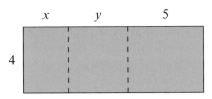

36 Expand the brackets in these expressions.

  a $5(p + q + 3)$ b $3(2a + b - 6)$

  c $4(12 - m + 2n)$ d $10(2h + 5 - k)$

  e $6(5 - 3c - 4d + 2e)$ f $3n(2p + 3q - 3)$

37 Expand the brackets and simplify these expressions.

  a $3(x + 5) + 2x$ b $4(2n - 3) - n$

  c $2(4 - 5t) + 6$ d $7(2a + 3) - 6a - 11$

  e $8(w + 2q) + w - 9q$ f $4h + 3(h + 5)$

38 Expand the brackets and simplify these expressions.

  a $5(3t + 1) + 4t + 3$ b $4(m + 2n + 3) + m + 4n + 6$

  c $14 + 3(7k + 2h + 5) - 9k - 10$ d $11 + 5x + 3(x + 2y) - 3y$

*39 Solve these equations by expanding the brackets first.

  a $3(x + 2.5) = 19.5$ b $4(x + 3) + 7 = 51$

  c $36 = 4(x + 3.5) + 6$ d $15 = x + 4(2x - 3)$

  e $3x + 2(x + 7) = 59$ f $5(x + 1) - 2x - 26 = 0$

*40 Three friends count how many marbles they have.
Paula has p marbles. Quentin has six fewer marbles than Paula.
Rachel has twice as many marbles as the other two have in total.

  a   How many marbles does Quentin have, in terms of p?

  b   Write an expression for the number of marbles that Rachel has.

  c   Write an expression for the total number of marbles. Simplify it.

  d   Paula, Quentin and Rachel have 48 marbles altogether.
Write an equation involving p.

  e   Solve your equation. How many marbles does Rachel have?

Functions and mappings

- Using algebra to describe a mapping
- Completing a mapping diagram

Keywords

You should know

explanation 1

1 **a** Copy and complete this mapping diagram to show $x \to 3x$.

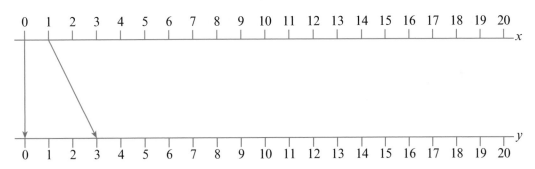

b Write the rule for the mapping as $y = \square$.

2 Here is a partly completed mapping diagram.

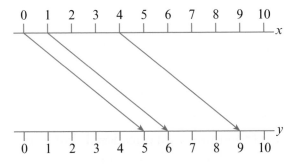

a Copy and complete the diagram.

b Copy and complete these statements.
The rule for the mapping may be written as

i $y = \square$ **ii** $x \to \square$

3 a Copy and complete this mapping diagram.

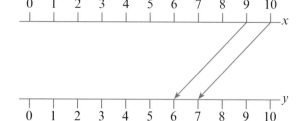

b Find the ouput for each of these input values.

   i 16   **ii** 21   **iii** 38

c Copy and complete these statements.
The rule for the mapping may be written as

   i $y = \square$ **ii** $x \rightarrow \square$

4 Here is a **function machine**. $x \rightarrow \boxed{\times 2} \rightarrow \boxed{+3} \rightarrow y$

a Copy and complete these statements.
The rule for the mapping may be written as

   i $y = \square$ **ii** $x \rightarrow \square$

b Find the **output** for each of these input values.

   i 0   **ii** 1   **iii** 4   **iv** 10

c Find the **input** for each of these output values.

   i 17   **ii** 63   **iii** 20   **iv** 50

d Copy and complete this mapping diagram.

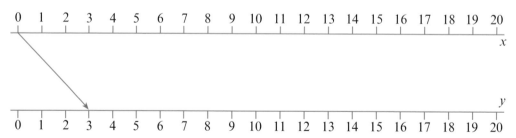

5 This function machine uses the same instructions as in question **1**, but in reverse order.

a Explain why the rule for this function machine cannot be written as $y = x + 3 \times 2$.

b Write the rule correctly in the form $y = \square$

c Find the value of y when $x = 10$.

d Find the value of x when $y = 50$.

*6 a   Which mapping diagram belongs to which equation?

 b   Copy and complete the mapping diagrams.

$$y = 20 - 2x \qquad y = 10 - x \qquad y = 2(x - 5) \qquad y = 2x - 5$$

$$y = 2x + 3 \qquad y = x - 1 \qquad y = x + 3$$

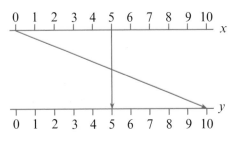

i
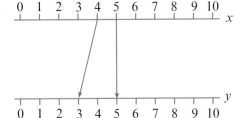

ii

iii

iv
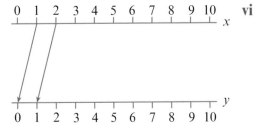

v

vi
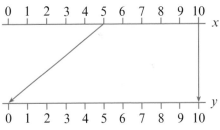

*7 a   Which of the labels below could match the partly completed mapping diagram?

 $x \rightarrow x$ $x \rightarrow 2(x - 2)$

$x \rightarrow 4x$ $x \rightarrow 8 - x$

 b   Which label is correct for each of these mappings?

   i $3 \rightarrow 5$ **ii** $10 \rightarrow 10$ **iii** $5 \rightarrow 6$

Measures

- Approximating sizes of everyday objects in metric units
- Reading scales on a variety of instruments
- Converting between different metric units

Keywords

You should know

explanation 1a   explanation 1b

1 Copy the table and put a tick in one column for each unit.
The first one has been done for you.

Unit	Length	Area	Capacity	Mass
Metre	✓			
Centilitre				
Centimetre				
Square millimetre				
Gram				
Litre				
Square centimetre				
Millimetre				
Kilogram				

2 The abbreviation for centimetre is cm. Write the abbreviation for each of the
following units.

   a millimetre   **b** centilitre   **c** square metre

   d square centimetre   **e** kilometre   **f** gram

   g metre   **h** kilogram   **i** millilitre

3 Copy and complete.

   a $10\,\text{mm} = 1\,\square$ **b** $100\,\square = 1\,\text{litre}$ **c** $1000\,\text{g} = 1\,\square$

   d $\square\,\text{cm} = 1\,\text{m}$ **e** $1000\,\square = 1\,\text{m}$ **f** $1000\,\square = 1\,\text{litre}$

4 What is the capacity of each container?

330 ml

2.5 litres

1 litre

100 ml

5 What is the mass of each item?

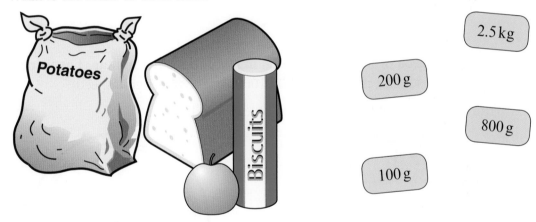

2.5 kg

200 g

800 g

100 g

6 Carol does her shopping on the internet.
She has to be careful to order things in the right quantities.
List any of the following items and quantities that don't seem to be correct.

Butter (500 g)   Milk (4 litres)
Cheese (400 g)   Potatoes (5 g)
Mushrooms (50 kg)   Broccoli (300 g)
Orange juice (1.5 ml)   Tomato sauce (330 litres)
Frozen peas (1.2 kg)   Carrots (2 kg)
Washing up liquid (500 litres)   Chocolate (100 g bar)

7 Write the value shown by each arrow.

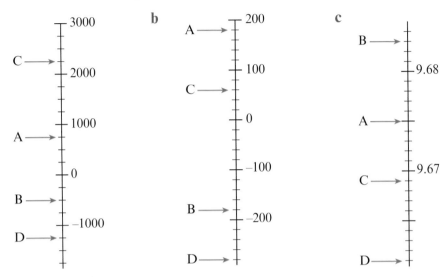

8 The engine speed of a car is measured in revolutions per minute. The value shown on these dials is multiplied by 1000 to give the engine speed.

Write down the engine speed shown on each dial.

a

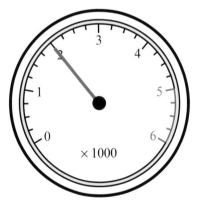

b

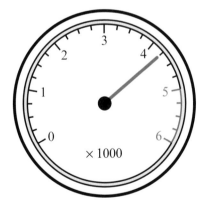

9 This dial shows the engine temperature of a car.

Estimate the temperature shown.

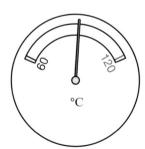

10 The temperature in a house is controlled by a thermostat.

Find the temperature set on each of these.

a 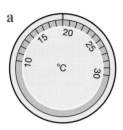 **b** 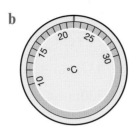 **c**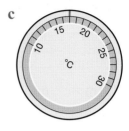

11 What is the size of the angles shown in these diagrams?

a

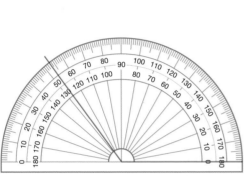

b

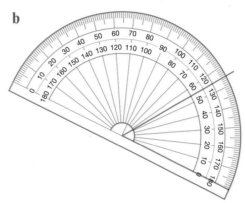

12 Read the values shown on these scales. Remember to include the units.

a

b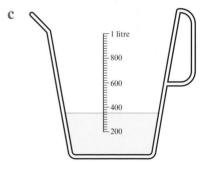

c

d

e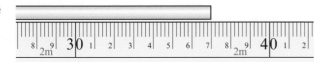

explanation 3

13 Copy and complete.

a $36\,cm = \square\,mm$

b $24.8\,cm = \square\,mm$

c $900\,mm = \square\,cm$

d $437\,mm = \square\,cm$

e $1.6\,m = \square\,mm$

f $320\,cm = \square\,m$

$$10\,mm = 1\,cm$$
$$100\,cm = 1\,m$$

14 Copy and complete.

a $75\,cl = \square\,litres$

b $2.5\,litres = \square\,ml$

c $125\,cl = \square\,litres$

d $330\,ml = \square\,cl$

e $3\,litres = \square\,cl$

f $55\,cl = \square\,ml$

$$10\,ml = 1\,cl$$
$$100\,cl = 1\,litre$$

15 Copy and complete.

a $2000\,g = \square\,kg$

b $3.5\,kg = \square\,g$

c $625\,g = \square\,kg$

d $0.7\,kg = \square\,g$

e $0.09\,kg = \square\,g$

f $24\,g = \square\,kg$

$$1000\,g = 1\,kg$$

16 Petrol is now sold in litres, but years ago it was sold by the gallon.
There are roughly 4.5 litres in 1 gallon.

a   A typical family car will travel
about 8 miles on 1 litre of fuel.
How many miles is this per gallon?

b   A Lamborghini will only travel
about 9 miles on 1 gallon of fuel.
How many miles is this per litre?

17 A standard ruler used in schools is 12 inches long.
What is the length of a standard ruler in centimetres?

1 inch is
about 2.5 cm.

18 Michael has a hand span of 20 cm. What is this in inches?

explanation 4a   explanation 4b   explanation 4c

19 How many hours are there in a week?

20 a How many minutes are there in a day?

b How many minutes are there in a week?

21 It has been calculated that Bill earns $250 per second.
How much does Bill earn in an hour?

22 Write these times using the 24-hour clock.

a 7:21 a.m.   b 3.20 p.m.   c 10:24 p.m.

d 5:15 p.m.   e 1:09 a.m.   f 1:36 p.m.

23 Write these times using the 12-hour clock.

a 18:05   b 16:22   c 09:20

d 11:30   e 23:55   f 10:42

24 Ben can walk to work in 22 minutes. He wants to arrive at
8:10 a.m. to prepare for a meeting. What time should Ben
leave for work?

25 Suzie is travelling from Stafford to Cambridge and has to change trains at
Nuneaton. Her arrival time at Nuneaton is 07:48 and her departure time is
08:03. How long does Suzie have to wait at Nuneaton?

26 The new high speed Channel Tunnel rail link makes it possible to travel from
London to Paris in 2 hours 15 minutes and from London to Brussels in
1 hour 51 minutes.

a A train leaves London at 14:47. What time will it arrive in Paris?

b A train arrives in Brussels from London at 16:24. What time did the train
leave London?

Triangles

- Recognising and naming different types of triangle
- Defining a triangle
- Constructing a triangle using SAS or ASA

Keywords

You should know

explanation 1a | explanation 1b | explanation 1c

1 The triangles in the diagram are drawn on isometric dotty paper.

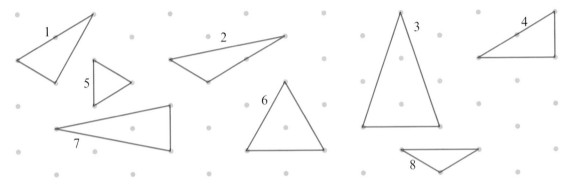

List the triangles that are

a equilateral b isosceles c right-angled

d obtuse-angled e scalene f acute-angled

2 Pick the best label for each of these triangles.

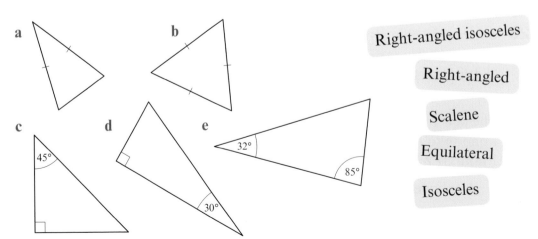

Right-angled isosceles

Right-angled

Scalene

Equilateral

Isosceles

3 A class was asked to draw a right-angled triangle ABC with AB = 4 cm and BC = 5 cm. The triangles that Saba and Abida drew are shown.

a Are the triangles the same?

b Who is right? Explain your answer.

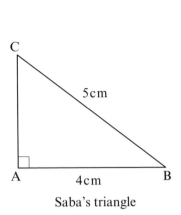

Saba's triangle

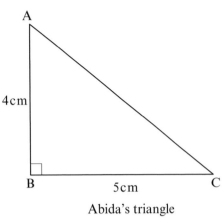

Abida's triangle

4 Use three letters to describe each of the angles shown in the diagram.

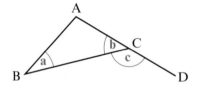

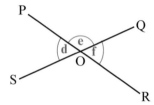

5 Here are two triangles ABC and XYZ.

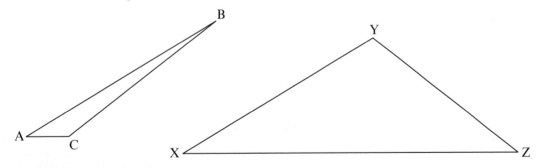

a Are the two triangles the same?

b Measure these lengths and angles.

i	AB	**ii**	XY	**iii**	BC
iv	YZ	**v**	Angle BAC	**vi**	Angle YXZ

c If you know the lengths of two sides of a triangle and one of its angles, is this always enough information to be able to draw that triangle?

135

explanation 2a explanation 2b explanation 2c

6 You are given the lengths of two sides of a triangle. Which angle do you need to know to complete the information for **SAS** when the given sides are

   a XY and YZ   **b** AC and AB   **c** PR and QR

> It's a good idea to sketch the triangles first.

7 a Use the information in these sketches to construct the triangles.

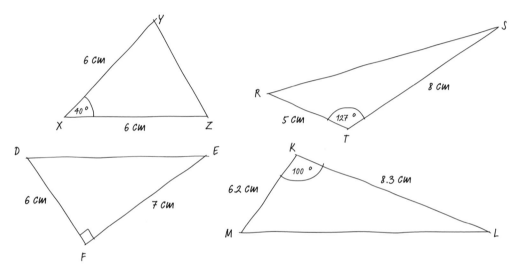

  b Measure these lengths and angles on your diagrams.

    i YZ   **ii** Angle XYZ   **iii** RS   **iv** Angle RST

    v DE   **vi** Angle EDF   **vii** ML   **viii** Angle KML

8 Construct triangle PQR where PQ = 7.3 cm, QR = 4.8 cm and angle PQR = 50°.

Measure PR and angle PRQ.

> Sketch the triangles first.

9 Construct triangle ABC where AC = 8.6 cm, AB = 3.9 cm and angle BAC = 120°.

Measure BC and angle ABC.

10 Construct triangle RST where RT = 5.7 cm, TS = 6.4 cm and angle RTS = 90°.

Measure RS and angle RST.

11 ABCD is a rhombus. AC and BD cross at their midpoints.

AC = 8 cm and BD = 6 cm.

Construct a triangle and use it to work out the perimeter of the rhombus. Explain how you did it.

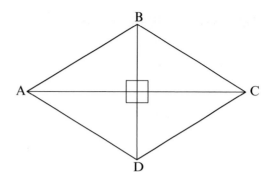

explanation 3a   explanation 3b   explanation 3c   explanation 3d

12 You are given the size of two angles in a triangle. Which side do you need to know to complete the information for **ASA** when the given angles are

    a ∠ABC and ∠ACB   **b** ∠FHG and ∠FGH   **c** ∠JKL and ∠KLJ

13 a Use the information in these sketches to construct the triangles.

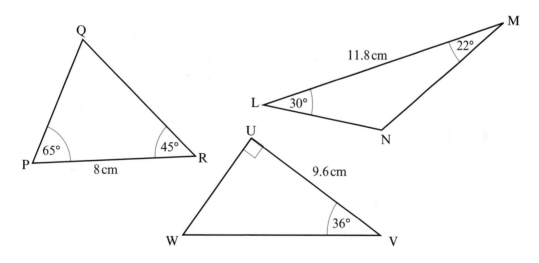

  b Find these lengths from your diagrams.

    i PQ   **ii** QR   **iii** UW   **iv** WV   **v** LN   **vi** MN

14 Construct triangle DEF where DE = 9.2 cm, ∠DEF = 45° and ∠FDE = 57°.

Measure DF.

15 Construct triangle KLM where LM = 11.3 cm, ∠KLM = 38° and ∠KML = 64°. Measure KL.

16 Construct triangle OPQ where OP = 7.4 cm, ∠QOP = 52° and ∠QPO = 41°. Measure PQ.

17 Daniel, Emily and Farah are trying to find the width of a river.
Emily stands to face Daniel on the opposite side of the river.
Farah measures 10 m along the river bank from Emily.
She measures the angle between the directions of Daniel and Emily as 53°.

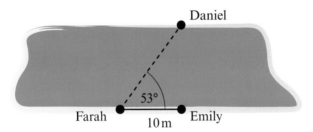

Construct a triangle to show this information. How wide is the river?

> You don't need to draw a line 10 m long! Use centimetres to represent metres.

18 The diagram shows two coastguard stations D and E, 8 km apart.
A distress flare F is sighted at the position shown.

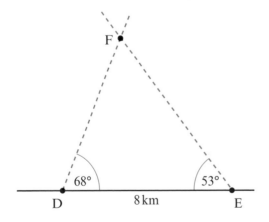

Construct a triangle using this information. Find the distance of the flare from each of the coastguard stations.

Nets and solid shapes

- Constructing a net for a solid shape
- Finding the surface area of a solid shape
- Relating the number of vertices, faces and edges of a solid shape

Keywords

You should know

explanation 1

1 a Which of these diagrams could be used as a net for a cube?

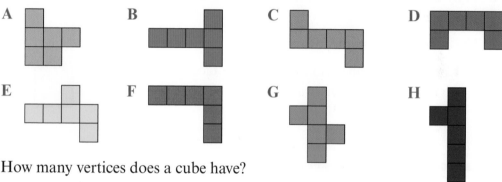

A   B   C   D

E   F   G   H

b How many vertices does a cube have?

c How many faces?

d How many edges?

2 The diagram shows a partly completed net for a cuboid drawn on a grid of 1 cm squares.

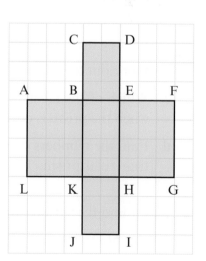

a What shape is needed to complete the net? Give its size.

b There are a number of options for where to place the missing part. List the edges where it could be attached.

c When the cuboid is made, which points will

i meet A   **ii** be furthest from E

d Give the dimensions of the completed cuboid.

e Find the area of each of these rectangles.

i ABKL   **ii** CDEB   **iii** BEHK

f Work out the total surface area of the cuboid.

139

3 The diagram shows a partly completed net for a cuboid on a grid of 1 cm squares.

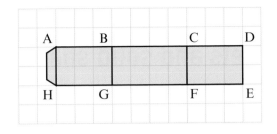

a Copy the diagram and complete it by drawing rectangles on the edges BC, DE and FE.

b The net has a flap on the edge AH.
How many flaps are needed altogether? Add the necessary flaps to your net.

c Work out the surface area of the cuboid.

4 Copy this net for a cube onto paper or card and add any necessary flaps.

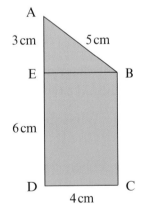

The cube is to be made into a dice.

a Complete the labels so that opposite faces add up to 7. In how many ways can this be done?

b Make the dice.

5 Here is a partly completed net for a triangular prism.

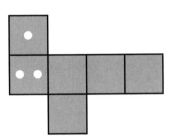

a Copy and complete the sketch by adding a triangle to the edge DC and rectangles to ED and BC. Include the measurements on your sketch.

b Work out the surface area of the triangular prism.

c Which of the labelled points will be furthest from A when the prism is complete?

d Find the numbers of vertices, faces and edges of a triangular prism.

6 Kay found the surface area of the prism in question **5** with this calculation.

$$3 \times 4 + 6(3 + 4 + 5)$$

a Explain why Kay's method works.

b Write an expression to find the surface area of a prism twice as long, but otherwise the same as the one in question **5**.

c Use your expression to calculate the surface area of this prism.

7 Here is a partly completed net of a triangular prism.

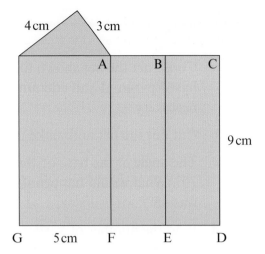

  a Write down the length of

    i AB   **ii** BC

  b Copy the net and complete it by adding a triangle to the edge GF. Label the lengths of its sides.

  c Repeat part **b** but, this time, attach the triangle to the edge FE.

  d Work out the surface area of the triangular prism.

8 Read the whole question before you do part **a**.

  a Use a ruler and protractor to construct the triangle shown.

    Check that each side is 3 cm long.

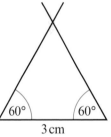

  b Use your triangle as part of a net for a triangular prism of length 5 cm.

  c Add flaps to your net and make the prism.

9 The diagram shows the net of a prism.

  a Which labelled point will be joined to A when it is complete?

  b Write down these lengths

    i AB   **ii** BC

    iii CD   **iv** DE

    v EF   **vi** FG

  c Copy and complete this expression for the surface area of the prism.

$$2(5^2 - \square^2) + \square(5 + \square + \square + \square + \square + \square)$$

  d What is the surface area?

  e Find the number of vertices, faces and edges of the prism.

  f What is the smallest shape that can be added to the prism to make a cuboid?

explanation 3

10 a Construct the net shown for a square-based pyramid and add any flaps as necessary.

b Cut out the net and make the pyramid.

c The angle at the base of the triangle is 70°. What would happen if this angle was 45°?

d Find the number of vertices, faces and edges of the pyramid.

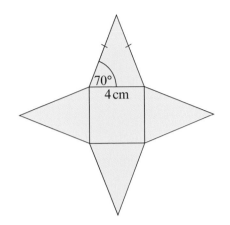

11 a Construct the triangle shown below.

b Join the midpoints of the sides to make the net of a tetrahedron and add the flaps.

c Cut out the net and fold to make the tetrahedron.

d Find the number of vertices, faces and edges of the tetrahedron.

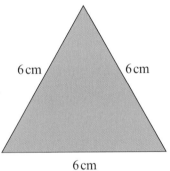

12 a Use your results from questions **1, 5, 9, 10** and **11** to complete the table.

Shape	Vertices (V)	Faces (F)	Edges (E)
Cube			
Triangular prism			
Prism			
Square-based pyramid			
Tetrahedron			

b Try to find a formula connecting the values of V, F and E.

13 Find the length of each edge of a cube if its surface area is

a $96 \, \text{cm}^2$ **b** $216 \, \text{cm}^2$ **c** $486 \, \text{cm}^2$

Geometry and measures GM3.4

Representing 3-D shapes

- Drawing solid shapes on plain paper
- Drawing solid shapes on isometric paper

Keywords

You should know

explanation 1a   explanation 1b

1 Write down the more usual name for each of these.

   a A circular-based pyramid   **b** A rectangular prism

   c A circular prism   **d** A triangular-based pyramid

2 Match each shape to its label.

Cone   Cylinder   Square-based pyramid   Cube

Triangular prism   Cuboid   Tetrahedron

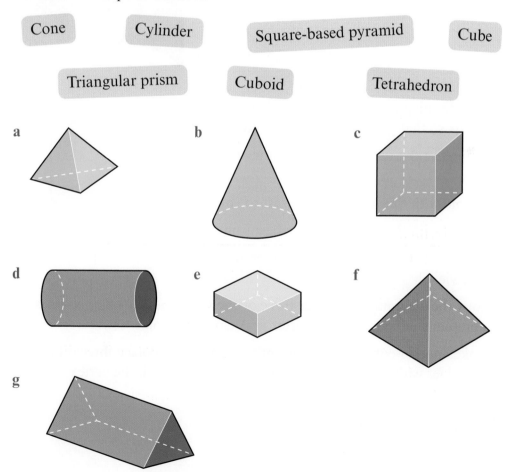

a

b

c

d

e

f

g

3 Here are some partly completed sketches of 3-D objects. Copy and complete them.

a 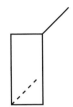   b 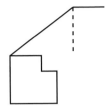   c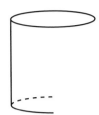

4 Look at the picture.

Can you see two faces?

Can you see a vase?

Can you switch between the two views?

5 Look at this diagram representing a shape made from glass so that you can see all of its edges.

It is actually a flat pattern of lines but try to visualise

- a cuboid with the vertex at A closest to you

- a cuboid with the vertex at A furthest from you

The hard part is to try to switch between the two possible views!

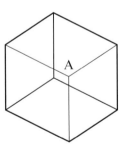

a   Copy the diagram but replace three of the solid lines with dotted lines to represent a cuboid with the vertex at A closest to you.

b   Make another copy of the diagram but, this time, replace three different solid lines with dotted lines to represent a cuboid with the vertex at A furthest from you.

6 This diagram represents a cone positioned slightly below your point of view.

Copy the diagram but make one change so that your point of view is slightly below the cone.

7 Look at this diagram representing a prism.

   a Does the shaded end appear closer or further away than the unshaded end?

   b Copy the diagram but change which lines are dotted so that the opposite end of the prism appears closer.

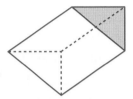

explanation 2

8 This diagram shows two cubes drawn on isometric dotty paper.

   a Copy the diagram and add an extra cube to make a block of three cubes in a straight line.

   b Is it easier to add the extra cube to the near end or the far end? Explain why.

9 a Copy this diagram and add an extra cube to make three cubes in a straight line.

   b Is it easier to add the extra cube to the near end or the far end?

10 This diagram shows one cube stacked on top of another.

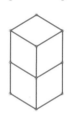

   a Copy the diagram an add a third cube to the stack.

   b Is it easier to add the third cube above or below the two cubes shown?

11 Eight cubes can be placed together to make a larger cube.

Show how this would look on isometric paper.

> Use your answers to questions 8, 9 and 10 to plan the order in which you draw the cubes.

12 Copy and complete this diagram to represent two layers of six cubes.

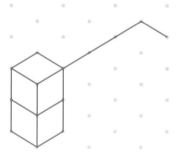

13 Copy and complete this drawing of a cuboid measuring 4 cm × 3 cm × 2 cm.

14 Use isometric paper to draw a cuboid with twice the dimensions of the one shown in the diagram below.

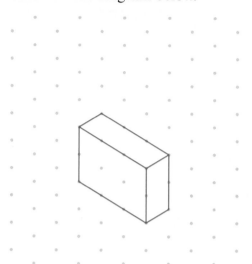

15 The diagram below shows shape A and a partly completed shape B.

The two shapes fit together to make a cuboid.

a Copy and complete shape B.

b Draw shape A with shape B in position to make the cuboid.

c What are the dimensions of the cuboid?

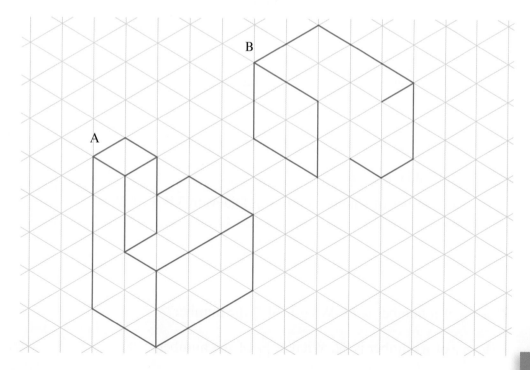

Fractions and percentages of amounts

- Calculating a fraction of an amount
- Calculating a percentage of an amount

Keywords

You should know

explanation 1

1 Here are some diagrams divided into smaller parts.

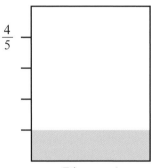 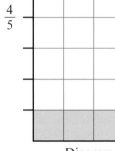 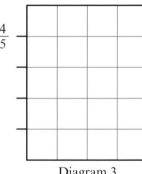

Diagram 1   Diagram 2   Diagram 3

a What fraction of Diagram 1 is blue?

b Copy Diagram 2 and write the missing fractions on the vertical scale.

c Copy and complete.

The number of blue squares in Diagram 2 is $\frac{\square}{\square}$ of 20 = $\frac{20}{\square}$

$= \square.$

d Copy Diagram 3 and shade $\frac{4}{5}$ of the squares.

e Copy and complete.

The number of shaded squares in Diagram 3 is $\frac{4}{5}$ of 20 = $\square \times \frac{1}{5}$ of 20

$= \square \times \square$

$= \square.$

2 a $\frac{1}{5}$ of a number is 23. What is of $\frac{2}{5}$ the number?

b $\frac{1}{11}$ of a number is 32. What is $\frac{3}{11}$ of the number?

3 a   i Copy and complete. $\frac{1}{3} = \frac{\square}{9}$

    ii $\frac{1}{9}$ of a number is 42. What is $\frac{1}{3}$ of the number?

  b   i Copy and complete. $1 = \frac{\square}{5}$

    ii $\frac{1}{5}$ of a number is 61. What is the number?

4 A man spent $\frac{1}{3}$ of each day sleeping.

He lived for 78 years.

How much time did he spend asleep?

5 Work out these amounts.

  a   i $\frac{1}{5}$ of 40   **ii** $\frac{2}{5}$ of 40   **iii** $\frac{3}{5}$ of 40

  b   i $\frac{1}{10}$ of 60   **ii** $\frac{3}{10}$ of 60   **iii** $\frac{7}{10}$ of 60

  c   i $\frac{1}{12}$ of 36   **ii** $\frac{5}{12}$ of 36   **iii** $\frac{11}{12}$ of 36

  d   i $\frac{1}{7}$ of 28   **ii** $\frac{2}{7}$ of 28   **iii** $\frac{5}{7}$ of 28

6 Write down the missing numbers.

  a $\frac{\square}{5}$ of 20 = 12   **b** $\frac{3}{8}$ of $\square$ = 21   **c** $\frac{11}{\square}$ of 24 = 22

  d $\frac{5}{\square}$ of 27 = 15   **e** $\frac{7}{20}$ of $\square$ = 35   **f** $\frac{\square}{50}$ of 200 = 52

7 Find the number of minutes in these fractions of an hour.

  a $\frac{1}{2}$ **b** $\frac{1}{4}$ **c** $\frac{3}{4}$

  d $\frac{5}{12}$ **e** $\frac{1}{6}$ **f** $\frac{5}{6}$

  g $\frac{2}{3}$ **h** $\frac{7}{10}$ **i** $\frac{2}{5}$

  j $\frac{4}{15}$ **k** $\frac{3}{5}$ **l** $\frac{9}{20}$

8 Find the number of degrees in these fractions of a turn.

a $\dfrac{1}{2}$ b $\dfrac{1}{3}$ c $\dfrac{1}{4}$

d $\dfrac{3}{4}$ e $\dfrac{2}{3}$ f $\dfrac{3}{10}$

g $\dfrac{5}{12}$ h $\dfrac{1}{5}$ i $\dfrac{4}{9}$

> There are 360° in a complete turn.

explanation 2a   explanation 2b

9 Work out these values.

a $\dfrac{2}{5} \times 30$ b $\dfrac{3}{4} \times 64$ c $\dfrac{6}{25} \times 75$

d $20 \times \dfrac{7}{10}$ e $32 \times \dfrac{11}{16}$ f $21 \times \dfrac{3}{7}$

10 Write the following as mixed numbers.

a $\dfrac{1}{3}$ of 8 b $15 \times \dfrac{1}{4}$ c $\dfrac{2}{3}$ of 11

d $\dfrac{3}{5} \times 9$ e $\dfrac{3}{4}$ of 21 f $44 \times \dfrac{5}{8}$

explanation 3

11 a Copy the diagram and fill in the missing values.

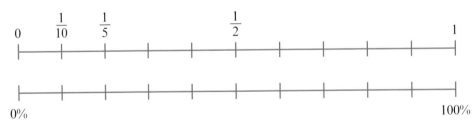

b Use your diagram to write these fractions as percentages.

i $\dfrac{1}{10}$ ii $\dfrac{3}{5}$ iii $\dfrac{9}{10}$ iv $\dfrac{2}{5}$

c Use your diagram to write these percentages as fractions.

i 20% ii 50% iii 70% iv 60%

12 Copy and complete.

a 30% of $40 = \dfrac{3}{\square}$ of 40

$= \square$

b 80% of $30 = \dfrac{\square}{\square}$ of 30

$= \square$

13 Work these out by writing the percentages as fractions.

a 20% of 60

b 50% of 86

c 25% of 36

d 10% of 3000

e 75% of 140

f 90% of 1200

g 40% of 65

h 25% of 24

i 60% of 25

explanation 4

14 Work these out and give your answers as decimals.

a 10% of 34

b 50% of 8.6

c 25% of 18

d 30% of 25

e 70% of 24

f 10% of 6.9

15 Find 10% of each of these amounts.

a   £80

b   £300

c   £1700

d   £25 000

e   £92

f   £7

g   £234

h   £67.50

i   £9.40

j   £27.80

k   £0.70

l   £1.50

16 Work out these values.

a 10% of £64

b 5% of £64

c 15% of £64

d 15% of £128

17 Work out these amounts.

a 10% of $46\,\text{kg}$

b 20% of $46\,\text{kg}$

c 30% of $46\,\text{kg}$

d 15% of $46\,\text{kg}$

e 10% of £24

f 5% of £24

g 2.5% of £24

h 17.5% of £24

i 50% of $60\,\text{m}$

j 5% of $60\,\text{m}$

k 45% of $60\,\text{m}$

l 55% of $60\,\text{m}$

m 50% of $84\,\text{g}$

n 25% of $84\,\text{g}$

o 12.5% of $84\,\text{g}$

> Look for ways to use one answer to work out another.

18 Use the methods of question **17** to work these out.

a   20% of £70   b   5% of 80 cm   c   25% of 140 mm

d   30% of £16   e   12.5% of 48 g   f   45% of 40 litres

g   15% of 32 km   h   7.5% of 120 people i   55% of 800 tonnes

19 a   Copy and complete.

$$3 \times 33\tfrac{1}{3} = 3(33 + \square)$$
$$= 99 + \square$$
$$= \square$$

b   Write $33\tfrac{1}{3}\%$ as a fraction in its lowest terms.

20 a   Find $33\tfrac{1}{3}\%$ of 21 m   b   Find $66\tfrac{2}{3}\%$ of 45 oz

21 A top sprinter can run at a speed of about 10 m/s.

A little-known fact is that some crocodiles can reach up to 40% of this speed.

How fast can these crocodiles run?

22 Find the sale price for each of these marked prices.

a   Coat £93   b   Jacket £45

c   Jeans £27   d   Shirt £36

e   Boots £57   f   Jumper £25.80

Sale
Everything
must go.

$33\tfrac{1}{3}\%$ off

23 A salesperson earns 15% commission on sales.

Find the commission earned on each of these amounts.

a   £340   b   £624   c   £2700

d   £84.60   e   £112.40   f   £99

24 A car costing £81 000 lost $66\tfrac{2}{3}\%$ of its value after 4 years.

What was it then worth?

Ratio and proportion

- Expressing a proportion as a fraction, decimal or percentage
- Comparing proportions
- Comparing two quantities using a ratio
- Simplifying a ratio and sharing an amount in a given ratio

Keywords

You should know

explanation 1

1 The proportions of the main gases that make the atmosphere on Earth are shown below. Unfortunately, they are mixed in with the proportions for the planet Mars.

Other 1%	Nitrogen 3%	Carbon dioxide 95%	Oxygen 21%	Nitrogen 78%	Other 2%

Copy and complete these tables by working out which information must go where.

We need oxygen to breathe ...

Planet	Gas	Proportion
Earth		
	Total	100%

Planet	Gas	Proportion
Mars		
	Total	100%

2 These diagrams are made from red and yellow squares.

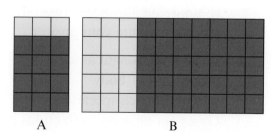

A   B

a Write down which diagram has

  i the most red squares

  ii the higher proportion of red squares

b Find the proportion of red squares in each diagram as

  i a fraction

  ii a percentage

3 In a football match, team A had 25 shots at goal with 17 on target.

Team B had 18 shots at goal with 12 on target.

a Write the proportion of shots on target for each team as a percentage.

b Which team seems to be more accurate?

4 Look at the statements written on these cards.

> Nine out of the top twenty fencers are left-handed.

> 82% of people are right-handed.

> Six of Europe's best ten table-tennis players are right-handed.

> Five out of the top twenty-five tennis players are left-handed.

a Use the statements to write the following proportions as percentages.

  i Left-handed people out of all people.

  ii Left-handed tennis players in the world's top twenty-five.

  iii Left-handed players among Europe's best ten table-tennis players.

  iv Left-handed fencers out of the top twenty in the world.

b What do your answers to part **a** suggest? Give a possible reason for this.

5 The table gives some information about typical brain weight and body weight for several species.

Species	Brain weight	Body weight
Dolphin	1700 g	170 000 g
Elephant	4000 g	4 000 000 g
Horse	420 g	350 000 g
Human	1400 g	70 000 g
Rabbit	12 g	2400 g
Rat	2.5 g	200 g

a Do you think that brain weight is a good way to compare intelligence across species? Explain your answer.

b Write brain weight as a proportion of body weight for each species. Give your answers as fractions in their lowest terms.

c Write the proportions found in part **b** as percentages.

d Use your answers to part **c** to list the species in order, highest first.

e Do you think that your list gives the species in order of intelligence? Explain your answer.

6 A typical tree shrew has a brain weight of 2.5 g and a body weight of 100 g.

  a What is brain weight as a proportion of body weight for the tree shrew as a percentage?

  b Compare this result with your answers to question **5**. What do you think this shows?

explanation 2a   explanation 2b

7 Danny and Nadia are going to share some sweets.

  a What is the ratio of blue sweets to orange sweets?

  b What is the ratio of orange sweets to blue sweets?

  c What is the ratio of blue sweets to the total number of sweets?

  d Danny eats one of the orange sweets.

  What is the new ratio of blue sweets to orange sweets in its simplest form?

  e Nadia then eats 3 sweets. This makes the ratio of blue sweets to orange sweets 2 : 1.

  How many blue sweets did Nadia eat?

8 Write each of these ratios in its simplest form.

a 8 : 12	**b** 27 : 9	**c** 24 : 30	**d** 30 : 25
e 62 : 31	**f** 24 : 32	**g** 7 : 21	**h** 45 : 30
i 42 : 56	**j** 120 : 270	**k** 55 : 132	**l** 68 : 51

9 Write each of these ratios in its simplest form.

   a £1:2p   **b** 25cm:1m   **c** 10cm:1mm

   d 1km:200m   **e** £1.45:£2.90   **f** 40mm:3cm

   g 16cm:1m   **h** 12mm:6cm   **i** 97m:97km

10 Find the missing quantities.

   a £2:$\Box$p = 4:1   **b** $\Box$mm:15cm = 1:5   **c** 3kg:$\Box$g = 50:1

   d $\Box$cm:1m = 2:5   **e** 0.5m:$\Box$cm = 2:1   **f** 1.2km:$\Box$m = 3:4

11 In a survey, 55% of students in their first year at university said that they could drive a car. Write the ratio of drivers to non-drivers in its simplest form.

12 5% of Swedish Finewool sheep are black and the rest are white. Write the ratio of black sheep to white sheep as simply as possible.

13 The ratio of occupied seats to empty seats for a theatre performance was 7:2. What fraction of the seats were empty?

14 An internet company found that $\frac{7}{8}$ of its customers had access to broadband. What is the ratio of broadband users to non-broadband users?

15 Yasmin mixes blue and yellow paint in the ratio 13:7 to make a shade of green.

   a What percentage of the paint Yasmin uses is yellow?

   b Find the amount of blue paint she should use to make the following amounts of green paint.

      i 60 litres   **ii** 140 litres   **iii** 10 litres

explanation 3

16 Asad and Sarah share £400 in the ratio 5:3. How much does each receive?

17 In the diagram, AP:PB = 8:5.

A   P   B

   a Find the distance AP if AB is 39 cm.

   b Find the distance PB if AB is 52 cm.

   c Find the distance AP if PB is 25 cm.

18 A shade of purple is made by mixing blue and red paint in the ratio 8:7.
Calculate the amount of each colour needed to make the following quantities.

   a 30 litres   **b** 75 litres   **c** 7.5 litres

19 The ratio of girls to boys on a school trip is 5:4.
Find the number of girls if there are

   a 56 boys   **b** 72 boys   **c** 189 pupils altogether

20 A red number and a blue number are hidden from view.

Seven times the red number is the same as nine times the blue number.

   a What is the ratio of the red number to the blue number?

   b Find the numbers if

      i their sum is 80   **ii** their difference is 120

Adding and subtracting fractions

- Adding fractions
- Subtracting fractions

Keywords

You should know

explanation 1

1 Copy and complete the fraction additions shown by these diagrams.

a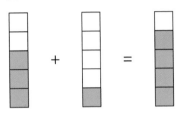

$$\frac{\square}{5} + \frac{\square}{5} = \frac{\square}{5}$$

b

$$\frac{\square}{5} + \frac{\square}{5} = \frac{\square}{5}$$

$$= \square$$

c

$$\frac{\square}{9} + \frac{\square}{\square} = \frac{\square}{\square}$$

d

$$\frac{\square}{\square} + \frac{\square}{\square} = \frac{\square}{\square}$$

$$= \frac{\square}{3}$$

d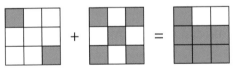

$$\frac{\square}{7} + \frac{\square}{\square} = \frac{\square}{\square}$$

f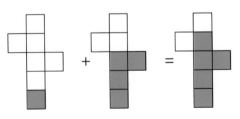

$$\frac{\square}{\square} + \frac{\square}{\square} = \frac{\square}{\square}$$

$$= \frac{\square}{2}$$

2 Copy and complete these diagrams and fraction calculations.

a 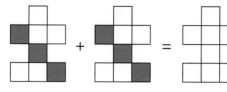　　b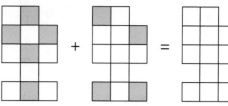

$$\frac{\square}{\square}+\frac{\square}{\square}=\frac{\square}{\square}$$

$$=\frac{\square}{4}$$

$$\frac{\square}{\square}+\frac{\square}{\square}=\frac{\square}{\square}$$

$$=\frac{3}{\square}$$

3 Simplify these as far as possible.

a　$\dfrac{5}{9}+\dfrac{2}{9}$　　　　b　$\dfrac{7}{12}+\dfrac{1}{12}$　　　　c　$\dfrac{3}{10}+\dfrac{5}{10}$

d　$\dfrac{7}{15}+\dfrac{5}{15}$　　　　e　$\dfrac{3}{16}+\dfrac{4}{16}+\dfrac{5}{16}$　　　　f　$\dfrac{2}{11}+\dfrac{6}{11}+\dfrac{3}{11}$

explanation 2

4 Copy and complete these diagrams and fraction calculations.

a 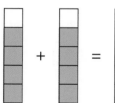　　b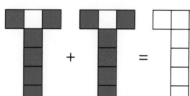

$$\frac{\square}{\square}+\frac{\square}{\square}=\frac{\square}{\square}$$

$$=\square\frac{\square}{\square}$$

$$\frac{\square}{\square}+\frac{\square}{\square}=\frac{\square}{\square}$$

$$=\square\frac{\square}{\square}$$

c 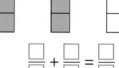　　d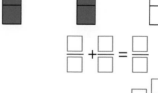

$$1\frac{\square}{\square}+\frac{\square}{\square}=\square\frac{\square}{\square}$$

$$=\square\frac{\square}{\square}$$

$$1\frac{\square}{\square}+\frac{\square}{\square}=\square\frac{\square}{\square}$$

$$=\square\frac{\square}{2}$$

5 Simplify these as far as possible.

a $\dfrac{7}{9} + \dfrac{6}{9}$

b $\dfrac{9}{12} + \dfrac{4}{12}$

c $\dfrac{2}{7} + \dfrac{5}{7}$

d $\dfrac{7}{8} + \dfrac{3}{8}$

e $\dfrac{4}{6} + \dfrac{5}{6}$

f $\dfrac{17}{20} + \dfrac{8}{20}$

6 Simplify these as far as possible.

a $1\dfrac{2}{5} + \dfrac{2}{5}$

b $1\dfrac{2}{5} + \dfrac{4}{5}$

c $1\dfrac{5}{8} + \dfrac{6}{8}$

d $1\dfrac{11}{12} + \dfrac{7}{12}$

e $2\dfrac{9}{10} + \dfrac{5}{10}$

f $3\dfrac{5}{6} + \dfrac{4}{6}$

explanation 3

7 Simplify these as far as possible.

a $\dfrac{8}{9} - \dfrac{5}{9}$

b $\dfrac{10}{12} - \dfrac{1}{12}$

c $\dfrac{13}{15} - \dfrac{3}{15}$

d $1 - \dfrac{2}{5}$

e $1 - \dfrac{7}{10}$

f $2 - \dfrac{3}{8}$

g $7 - \dfrac{4}{11}$

h $9 - \dfrac{3}{20}$

i $16 - \dfrac{9}{25}$

8 Simplify these as far as possible.

a $1\dfrac{1}{3} - \dfrac{2}{3}$

b $1\dfrac{1}{4} - \dfrac{3}{4}$

c $2\dfrac{4}{9} - \dfrac{7}{9}$

explanation 4

9 Copy and complete this diagram and fraction calculation.

$$\dfrac{\square}{5} + \dfrac{\square}{\square} = \dfrac{\square}{10} + \dfrac{\square}{\square}$$

$$= \dfrac{\square}{\square}$$

10 Copy and complete these diagrams and fractions calculations.

a  –  =

$$\frac{\square}{\square} - \frac{\square}{3} = \frac{\square}{\square} - \frac{\square}{\square}$$

$$= \frac{\square}{\square}$$

b + 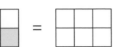 =

$$\frac{\square}{\square} + \frac{\square}{\square} = \frac{\square}{\square} + \frac{\square}{\square}$$

$$= \square\frac{\square}{\square}$$

*11 Simplify these fraction calculations as far as possible.

a $\frac{1}{2} + \frac{3}{8}$ b $\frac{3}{4} + \frac{7}{16}$ c $\frac{11}{12} - \frac{1}{6}$

d $\frac{17}{20} + \frac{4}{5}$ e $\frac{11}{15} - \frac{2}{3}$ f $\frac{9}{25} - \frac{14}{75}$

*12 Simplify these fraction calculations as far as possible.

a $\frac{9}{10} + \frac{3}{5}$ b $\frac{5}{6} + \frac{7}{24}$ c $\frac{41}{50} + \frac{6}{25}$

d $2\frac{3}{5} + \frac{1}{10}$ e $3\frac{7}{12} - \frac{1}{3}$ f $9\frac{1}{4} - \frac{5}{12}$

g $\frac{9}{10} + \frac{7}{20} + \frac{3}{5}$ h $\frac{2}{3} + \frac{7}{12} - \frac{1}{6}$ i $\frac{23}{25} - \frac{9}{50} + \frac{7}{10}$

*13 Tara spends $\frac{1}{5}$ of her pocket money on sweets and $\frac{2}{3}$ on clothes. She saves the rest.

What proportion of her pocket money does Tara save?

Sweets Clothes Save

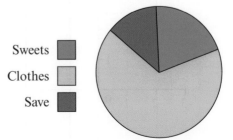

Algebra A4.1

Functions and graphs

- Plotting and drawing the graph of an equation
- Recognising the graph of an equation

Keywords

You should know

explanation 1

1 a Write down the coordinates of the points A, B, C and D.

b Describe in words what the coordinates have in common.

c What is the equation of the line?

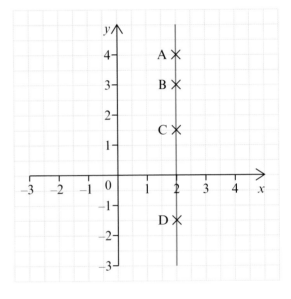

2 Write down the equation of the lines a, b and c.

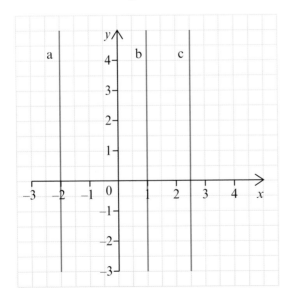

3 **a** Write the coordinates of A, B, C and D.

  b Write the equation of the line containing the labelled points.

  c Write the equations of lines i and ii.

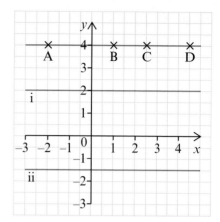

4 **a** Write down the equations of lines i and ii.

  b What are the coordinates of the point where the lines intersect?

  c Write the coordinates of the points where these pairs of lines intersect.

   i $x = 7$ and $y = 3$

   ii $x = -2$ and $y = 4$

   iii $x = 3.5$ and $y = -1$

   iv $x = -1.5$ and $y = -9$

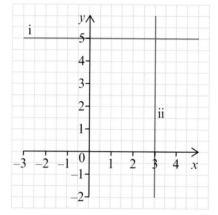

explanation 2a   explanation 2b

5 **a** Copy these axes and draw the line $y = x$. Write the equation next to the line.

  b Copy and complete the table for the equation $y = x + 1$.

x	−4	−3	−2	−1	0	1	2	3
y	−3							

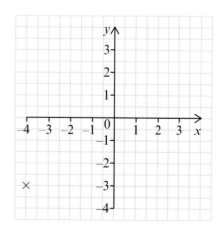

  c Plot the x, y pairs from the table as coordinates.

  d Draw the line $y = x + 1$ through your plotted points. Write the equation next to the line.

  e Compare the line $y = x + 1$ to the line $y = x$.

Your plotted points should lie on a straight line.

163

6 a Copy and complete these coordinates of points on the line
$y = x + 2$.

    i $(-4, \square)$ **ii** $(0, \square)$ **iii** $(2, \square)$

b Plot the points on the diagram used for question **5**.

c Draw and label the line $y = x + 2$.

d Draw and label the line $y = x + 3$.

e Draw and label the line $y = x - 1$.

> explanation 3

7 Find the coordinates of A, B, C and D in these sketches.

a 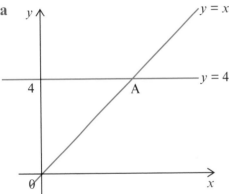   **b**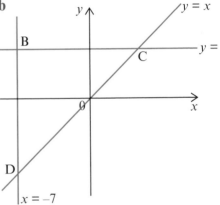

8 Sketch the graphs of $y = x - 2$, $x = 3$ and $y = 5$ on the same diagram.

Find the coordinates of the points of intersection of these lines.

    a $y = x - 2$ and $x = 3$ **b** $x = 3$ and $y = 5$ **c** $y = x - 2$ and $y = 5$

9 Find the coordinates of the points where the following lines intersect.

    a $x = 3$ and $y = x$ **b** $x = -2$ and $y = x$

    c $y = 5$ and $y = x$ **d** $y = x$ and $y = -4$

    e $y = x + 1$ and $x = 3$ **f** $y = x - 4$ and $x = -2$

> You may find it helpful to sketch the graphs.

10 a Copy and complete the table for the equation $y = 2x$.

x	0	1	2	3	4	5
y	0					

b Plot the values from your table as coordinates on a copy of the axes shown.

c Draw and label the line $y = 2x$.

d Which point do the lines $y = x$ and $y = 2x$ have in common?

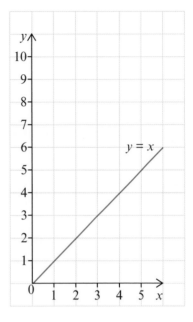

11 a Explain why any line of the form $y = mx$, where m is a fixed number, must pass through the origin.

b Find the value of y when $x = 2$ for each of these equations.

   i $y = 3x$ **ii** $y = 4x$ **iii** $y = 5x$ **iv** $y = \frac{1}{2}x$

c Add the graphs of the equations in part **b** to the diagram from question **10**. Label each graph with its equation.

d Describe how changing the value of m affects the graph of $y = mx$.

12 a Copy and complete the table for the equation $y = 2x + 3$.

x	0	1	2	3	4
y	3				

b Draw the line $y = 2x + 3$.

c Write down the coordinates of the point where the line crosses

   i the x-axis   **ii** the y-axis

13 a Copy and complete the table for the equation $y = 5 - x$.

x	−2	−1	0	1	2	3
y	7					

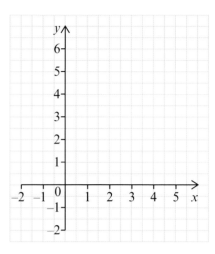

b Plot the values from your table as coordinates on a copy of the axes shown.

c Draw and label the line $y = 5 - x$.

d Write the coordinates of the points where the line crosses each axis.

14 a Copy and complete the following coordinates of points on the line $y = 4 - x$.
 i (−2, ☐)   **ii** (1, ☐)   **iii** (5, ☐)

b Plot the points on the diagram used for question **13**.

c Draw and label the line $y = 4 - x$.

d Write the coordinates of the points where the line crosses each axis.

15 a Write the equation of each of the labelled lines.

b Copy the diagram and add a sketch of the line $y = x$.

c Write the coordinates of the points where the line $y = x$ crosses each line.

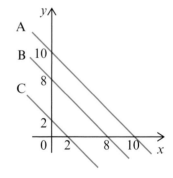

16 Here are some equations.

$y = x$

$x = -2$

$y = 4$

$y = 2 - x$

$y = x + 1$

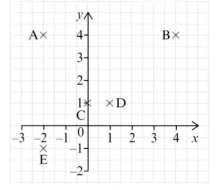

Match each pair of points to an equation.

a A and B   **b** A and E

c B and D   **d** E and C

e A and D

Algebra A4.2

Using graphs

- Using graphs to convert one quantity into another
- Using graphs to solve equations

Keywords

You should know

explanation 1

1 A teacher uses this graph to convert test marks to percentages.

a Use the red lines to help you write a mark of 21 as a percentage.

b Write these marks as percentages.

  i 28   ii 14   iii 17.5

c What was the highest possible test mark?

d The lowest percentage scored was 20%. How many marks did this person score?

e The highest percentage scored was 90%. How many marks did this person score?

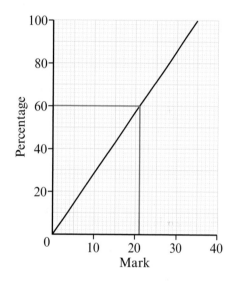

2 You can use this graph to convert between inches (in) and centimetres (cm).

a Write these measurements to the nearest inch.

  i 20 cm   ii 90 cm

  iii 55 cm   iv 32 cm

b Write these measurements to the nearest centimetre.

  i 12 in   ii 20 in   iii 30 in   iv 16 in

c Write these measurements in order of size, smallest first.

  21 in, 46 cm, 49.2 cm, 19 in

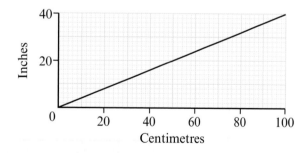

3 You can use this graph to convert between temperatures in degrees
Celsius (°C) and degrees Fahrenheit (°F).

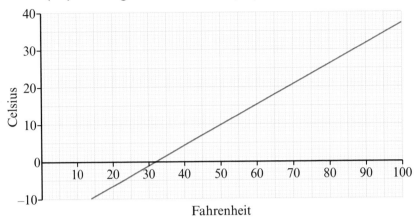

a A typical classroom temperature is around 20°C. Write this in Fahrenheit.

b On a summer's day, the temperature might be 86°F. Write this in Celsius.

c At what temperature in Fahrenheit does the graph cross the horizontal axis?

d The temperature one morning in winter is −5°C. Write this in Fahrenheit.

e Human body temperature is 98.4°F. Write this in Celsius to the nearest degree.

4 10 kg is approximately 22 lb and this is shown by the cross on the diagram.

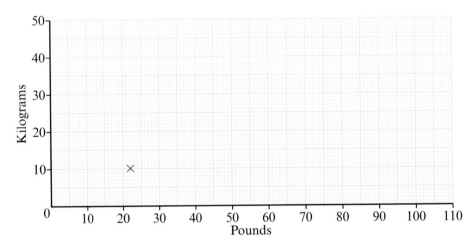

a Copy the diagram. Plot three more points. Draw a graph through the
plotted points.

b Copy and complete these conversions to the nearest whole number.

 i   15 kg = ☐ lb   **ii**   45 kg = ☐ lb

 iii 37 lb = ☐ kg   **iv**   101 lb = ☐ kg

explanation 2

5 The diagram shows the graph of $y = 2x - 3$.

   a Use the red lines to help you solve the equation
   $2x - 3 = 5$.

   b Use the graph to solve these equations.

   i $2x - 3 = 1$ **ii** $2x - 3 = 0$

   iii $2x - 3 = -3$ **iv** $2x - 3 = -1$

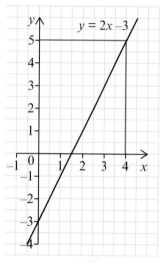

6 The diagram shows the graph of $y = \frac{1}{2}x + 5$.

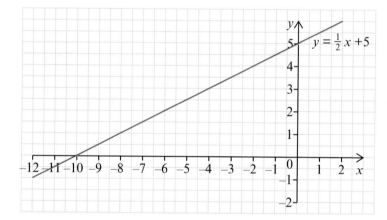

   a Use the graph to solve these equations.

   i $\frac{1}{2}x + 5 = 4$ **ii** $\frac{1}{2}x + 5 = 1$ **iii** $\frac{1}{2}x + 5 = 0$

   iv $\frac{1}{2}x + 5 = 2.5$ **v** $\frac{1}{2}x + 5 = 5$ **vi** $\frac{1}{2}x + 5 = -1$

   b Which equation in part **a** is equivalent to the equation $\frac{1}{2}x + 17 = 16$?

   c Copy and complete. $\frac{1}{2}x + 21 = 19.5$

$$\frac{1}{2}x + 5 = \square$$
$$x = \square$$

7 a Copy and complete the table for the equation $y = 10 - 4x$.

x	-1	0	1
y	14		

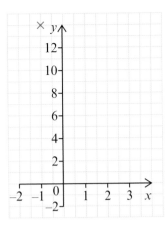

b Plot the points and use them to draw the line $y = 10 - 4x$.

c Use your graph to solve these equations.

    i $10 - 4x = 2$ **ii** $10 - 4x = 0$

    iii $10 - 4x = 4$ **iv** $10 - 4x = -2$

8 a Copy and complete the table for the equation $y = \dfrac{x + 3}{2}$.

x	-5	0	5
y	-1		

b Plot the points and use them to draw the line $y = \dfrac{x + 3}{2}$.

c Use your graph to solve these equations.

    i $\dfrac{x + 3}{2} = 3$ **ii** $\dfrac{x + 3}{2} = 1.5$ **iii** $\dfrac{x + 3}{2} = 0$

    iv $\dfrac{x + 3}{2} = 2$ **v** $\dfrac{x + 3}{2} = 3.5$ **vi** $\dfrac{x + 3}{2} = -0.5$

d Copy and complete. $\dfrac{x + 3}{2} + 7 = 6$

$$\dfrac{x + 3}{2} = \square$$

$$x = \square$$

9 a Copy and complete the table for the equation $v = 3 - \dfrac{t}{2}$.

t	0	2	4
v			

b Draw the graphs of $v = 3 - \dfrac{t}{2}$ and $v = t$ on the same axes.

c Solve the equation $3 - \dfrac{t}{2} = 0$.

d Use your graphs to solve the equation $t = 3 - \dfrac{t}{2}$.

Reflection

• Reflecting points and lines in a variety of mirror lines

Keywords

You should know

explanation 1

1 Copy these diagrams and show the image of each labelled point after reflection in the black mirror lines. Label the images A', B', C', D' and E'.

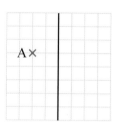 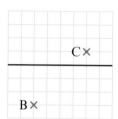 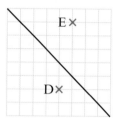

2 Copy these diagrams and draw a mirror line in the correct position for each one.

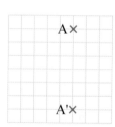 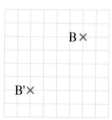 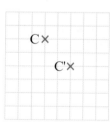

explanation 2

3 Copy the diagrams and reflect each labelled line in the black mirror line. Label the end points of each reflection.

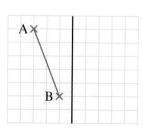 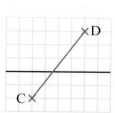 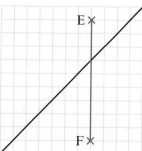

4 Copy these diagrams and reflect each shape in the black mirror line.

a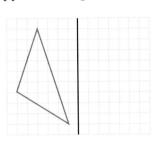

b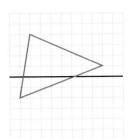

c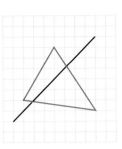

explanation 3

5 The image of A(3, 1) after reflection in the line $x = 4$ is A'(5, 1).

Write down the image of each of the other labelled points after reflection in $x = 4$.

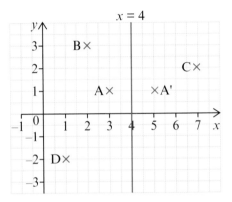

6 Write down the equation of the mirror line for each of the following.

a $A \rightarrow B$

b $B \rightarrow C$

c $B \rightarrow D$

d $B \rightarrow E$

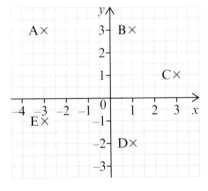

7 Write down the coordinates of a point that maps to itself after reflection in $x = 2$.

8 Write down the coordinates of the point that (3, −1) maps to after reflection in each of these lines.

a $x = 5$

b $x = -1$

c $y = -1$

d $y = 4$

e $y = x$

f $y = 2 - x$

g $y = -x$

h $y = 4 - x$

Rotation

- Describing a rotation
- Rotating a shape using tracing paper
- Rotating a shape on a rectangular grid
- Mapping one point to another under a rotation

Keywords

You should know

explanation 1

1 Copy this diagram. Show the new position of the shape after a 90° clockwise rotation with these centres.

a P   b Q

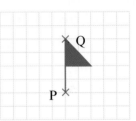

2 Copy these diagrams. Show the new position of each shape after an anticlockwise rotation of 90° with centre P.

a 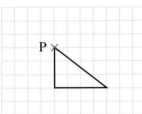   b 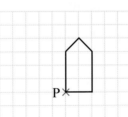   c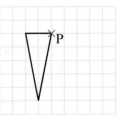

3 Copy these diagrams. Show the new position of each shape after a clockwise rotation of 90° with centre P.

a 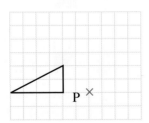   b 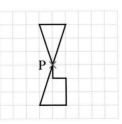   c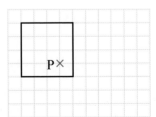

4 Copy this diagram and rotate the triangle through 180° with centre P.

Explain why it isn't necessary to give the direction of rotation.

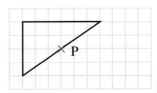

173

5 Describe the rotation that maps shape A to shape B in each of these diagrams.

a
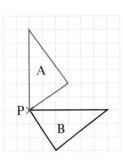

b
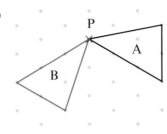

Every line of shape A is rotated through the same angle to make shape B.

Choose the simplest pair of matching lines to work out the angle.

6 The triangle shown here is rotated through 90° clockwise so that A→ A'.

Copy the diagram and draw the triangle in its new position.

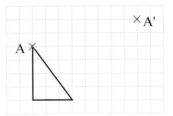

7 Copy this diagram.

a Rotate triangle A through 90° clockwise about (0, 0). Label the image B.

b Rotate triangle A through 90° anticlockwise about (0, 0). Label the image C.

c Rotate triangle A through 180° about (0, 0). Label the image D.

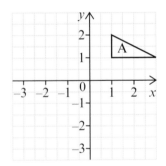

8 Describe these rotations.

a A→ B

b A→ C

c B→ D

d C→ D

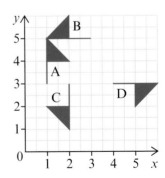

9 Triangle ABC has coordinates A(2, −1), B(4, 1) and C(−1, 3).

The triangle is rotated through 180° with centre (0, 0) to make triangle A' B' C'.

Find the coordinates of A', B' and C'.

Translation

- Describing a translation
- Applying a translation to a shape
- Using coordinates to describe a translation

Keywords

You should know

explanation 1

1 Describe these translations.

   a A→B   **b** A→C

   c B→A   **d** C→A

   e D→A   **f** A→E

   g A→D   **h** E→A

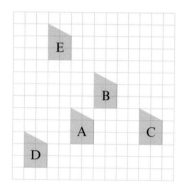

2 P is mapped to Q by the translation 3 units right and 2 units down.

Describe the translation that maps Q to P.

3 In this diagram, each triangle can be mapped to one other triangle by a translation.

For each of the following

   i copy and complete the mapping

   ii describe the translation.

   a A → ☐   **b** ☐ → F

   c J → ☐   **d** ☐ → I

   e B → ☐

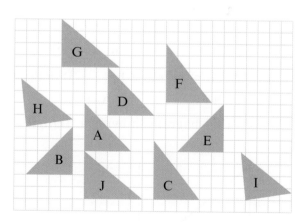

4 Triangle ABC is mapped to triangle A'B'C' by a translation.

   a Write down the coordinates of A and A'.

   b Describe the translation.

   c Find the coordinates of B' and C'.

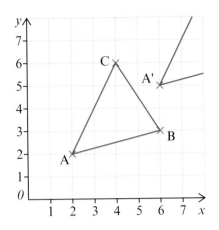

5 Triangle XYZ is mapped to triangle X'Y'Z' by a translation.

   a Describe the translation.

   b Find the coordinates of X' and Z'.

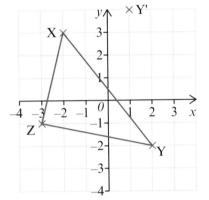

6 A translation maps (3, 7) to (5, 2).

   a Describe the translation.

   b Find the image of these points under the same translation.

   i (1, 9)   **ii** (−1, 6)   **iii** (−4, −2)

   c Which point maps to (3, −3) under this translation?

7 Copy this diagram showing a triangle and two mirror lines M_1 and M_2.

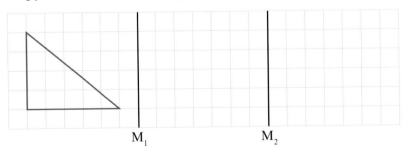

   a Reflect the triangle in M_1.   **b** Reflect the image in M_2.

   c Describe the translation equivalent to the two reflections.

Comparing data

- Comparing data using charts
- Comparing data using an average and the range

Keywords

You should know

explanation 1a   explanation 1b

1   Luca is the entertainment manager at a holiday resort.

He has some pie charts that show him the age profiles of the people on holiday.

Each chart below shows the proportion of holidaymakers in each age group in a single month.

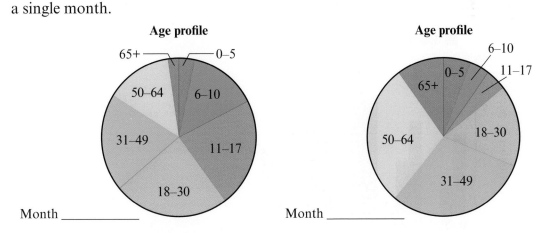

Unfortunately, he isn't sure which months they refer to!

He knows that one is for May and one is for July.

a   Compare the charts and describe the main differences.

b   Which chart do you think represents July?
   Explain how you were able to decide.

c   On the second chart, the 18–30 class has a larger angle than the 11–17 class.
   What does this mean?

d   The 31–49 class shown on the first chart has a smaller angle than the 31–49 class shown on the second chart. Does this mean that it contains fewer people?
   Explain your answer.

explanation 2

2 Sarah and Rifat have been running. Their trainer records their pulse rates every minute during the next few minutes.

> Your pulse rate increases with exercise and reduces again as you recover.

Sarah's median pulse rate is 120 with a range of 70.

Rifat's median pulse rate is 130 with a range of 40.

a Suggest possible values of the highest and lowest pulse rates for each runner.

b Who do you think had the lower pulse rate at the end of the run? Explain your answer.

c Who is showing the greater rate of recovery? Explain your answer.

3 This chart shows two sets of test results for a group of pupils.

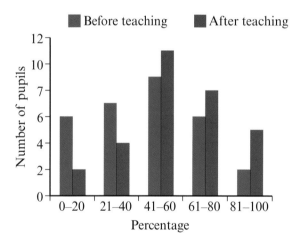

The first test was given during the introduction to a topic.

The second test was given after the topic had been taught.

a Compare the performance of pupils in the two tests.

Is the mean score in the second test greater or less than the mean score in the first test?

b What is the modal class for each test?

Do you think that the modal class is a useful way of measuring the difference between the two sets of scores?

c Is it possible for the range of scores to be the same in both tests? Explain your answer.

4 This diagram shows a section of dual carriageway passing through a village.

● Speed camera   ▬▬ Dual carriage way
                         ▬▬ Minor road

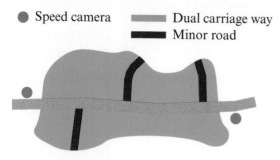

The speed limit is 40 mph, but many motorists did not slow down. The villagers were concerned about safety.

A survey found that the mean speed of cars on the dual carriageway was 53 mph. The range of speeds was 32 mph.

Police then set up speed cameras, as shown by red dots, and put up signs to warn motorists.

   a What effect do you think this had?

   b Explain the likely effect on the mean speed and range.

   c What would you expect the modal speed to be? Explain your answer.

5 A group of pupils each made a five-sided spinner for a probability experiment.

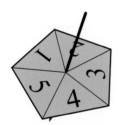

Each pupil carried out ten spins and recorded how many 4s they scored.

   a Mark scored three 4s from ten spins.

       Write this as a percentage of the number of spins in the trial.

   b Approximately how many 4s should each pupil expect from ten spins?

   c Write your answer to part **b** as a percentage.

   d Approximately what percentage of 4s would you expect from twenty spins?

       The group recorded their results in the table shown on the next page.

e   Copy the table and fill in the missing values.

Number of 4s in ten spins	Percentage of 4s	Frequency	Percentage × Frequency
0	0	3	
1	10	8	
2	20	9	
3	30	6	
4	40	3	
5	50	1	
		Total:	Total:

The *frequency* tells you how many pupils scored the number of 4s shown in the first column.

Three pupils got no 4s, eight pupils got one 4, nine pupils got two 4s, and so on.

f   Use the table to work out the mean of the percentages to 1 decimal place.

g   Write down the range of the percentages.

h   This table shows the results after each pupil has done 20 spins. Copy it and fill in the missing values.

Number of 4s in twenty spins	Percentage of 4s	Frequency	Percentage × Frequency
1	5	2	
2	10	3	
3	15	6	
4	20	7	
5	25	7	
6	30	3	
7	35	2	
		Total:	Total:

i   Work out the new mean to 1 decimal place.

j   Work out the new range.

k   Look at how the mean and range values have changed.

What do you think might happen to the mean and range if the number of spins is increased more and more?

Using statistics

- Applying your knowledge of statistics to solve problems

Keywords

You should know

explanation 1a   explanation 1b

This is an example of a simple question to investigate, although there are other things you have to consider before you can begin the investigation.

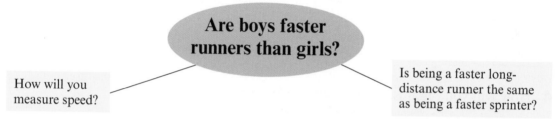

An example of a more complicated question is shown below.
There are lots of different things you can investigate to answer this question.
A sample of these smaller investigations is shown here.

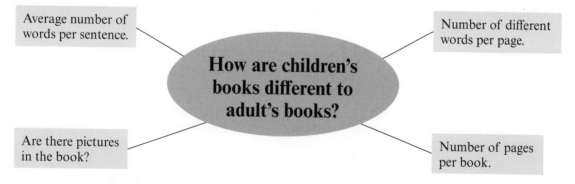

1 Choose a question to investigate. You could investigate one of the examples above or find an example of your own.
Can you answer your question with a single investigation or does it have lots of smaller questions to answer?

explanation 2a   explanation 2b

2 What sort of data can you collect for your question?

Will you use primary data or secondary data? You might need to use more than one sort of data to answer your question.

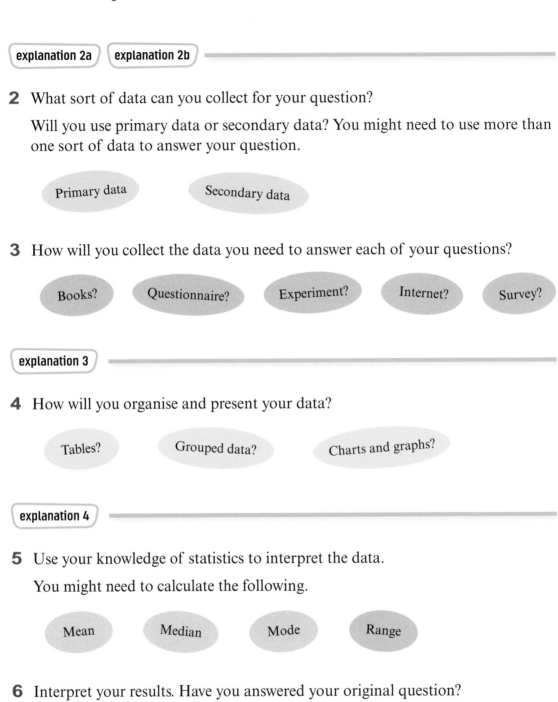

Primary data   Secondary data

3 How will you collect the data you need to answer each of your questions?

Books?   Questionnaire?   Experiment?   Internet?   Survey?

explanation 3

4 How will you organise and present your data?

Tables?   Grouped data?   Charts and graphs?

explanation 4

5 Use your knowledge of statistics to interpret the data.

You might need to calculate the following.

Mean   Median   Mode   Range

6 Interpret your results. Have you answered your original question?

7 Display your work.

Fractions of integers

- Using a diagram to multiply a fraction by an integer
- Multiplying a fraction by an integer without a diagram
- Cancelling when multiplying a fraction by an integer

Keywords

You should know

explanation 1a   explanation 1b

1 Copy and complete the fraction calculations to match the diagrams.

a

$\dfrac{1}{7}$

$\square \times \dfrac{\square}{7}$ $\dfrac{1}{7}$ $\dfrac{1}{7}$ $\dfrac{1}{7}$ $\dfrac{1}{7}$ $\dfrac{1}{7}$ $\dfrac{1}{7}$

$= \dfrac{\square}{7}$ $\dfrac{1}{7}$ $\dfrac{1}{7}$ $\dfrac{1}{7}$ $\dfrac{1}{7}$ $\dfrac{1}{7}$ $\dfrac{1}{7}$

b

$\dfrac{1}{5}$

$\square \times \dfrac{\square}{5}$ $\dfrac{1}{5}$ $\dfrac{1}{5}$ $\dfrac{1}{5}$ $\dfrac{1}{5}$ $\dfrac{1}{5}$ $\dfrac{1}{5}$ $\dfrac{1}{5}$ $\dfrac{1}{5}$

$= \square \dfrac{\square}{5}$ $\dfrac{1}{5}$ $\dfrac{1}{5}$ $\dfrac{1}{5}$ $\dfrac{1}{5}$ $\dfrac{1}{5}$ $\dfrac{1}{5}$ $\dfrac{1}{5}$ $\dfrac{1}{5}$

c

$\dfrac{1}{3}$

$\square \times \dfrac{2}{\square} = \dfrac{\square}{\square}$ $\dfrac{1}{3}$ $\dfrac{1}{3}$ $\dfrac{1}{3}$ $\dfrac{1}{3}$ $\dfrac{1}{3}$ $\dfrac{1}{3}$ $\dfrac{1}{3}$ $\dfrac{1}{3}$

$= \square \dfrac{\square}{\square}$ $\dfrac{1}{3}$ $\dfrac{1}{3}$ $\dfrac{1}{3}$ $\dfrac{1}{3}$ $\dfrac{1}{3}$ $\dfrac{1}{3}$ $\dfrac{1}{3}$ $\dfrac{1}{3}$

2 Copy and complete.

a $2 \times \dfrac{3}{7} = \dfrac{\Box \times \Box}{7}$

$= \dfrac{\Box}{7}$

b $4 \times \dfrac{2}{5} = \dfrac{\Box \times \Box}{5}$

$= \dfrac{\Box}{5}$

$= \Box \dfrac{\Box}{5}$

c $2 \times \dfrac{4}{9} = \dfrac{\Box \times \Box}{9}$

$= \dfrac{\Box}{9}$

d $3 \times \dfrac{5}{8} = \dfrac{\Box \times \Box}{8}$

$= \dfrac{\Box}{8}$

$= \Box \dfrac{\Box}{8}$

3 Work out these fractions.

a $2 \times \dfrac{2}{3}$

b $3 \times \dfrac{4}{7}$

c $5 \times \dfrac{3}{8}$

d $4 \times \dfrac{5}{9}$

e $\dfrac{3}{5}$ of 6

f $9 \times \dfrac{1}{3}$

g $\dfrac{2}{11}$ of 12

h $9 \times \dfrac{3}{10}$

i $\dfrac{4}{17}$ of 5

4 A snail, travelling at top speed, can cover about $\dfrac{2}{3}$ m in one hour.

How far would a snail travel in four hours at this speed?

5 A drinks supplier sells $\dfrac{3}{4}$ million cans of fizzy drink each day.

How many cans are sold in five days?

6 This square ABCD has area 14 cm².

Work out the area of the shaded part.

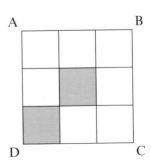

explanation 2

7 Copy and complete.

a $12 \times \dfrac{5}{8} = \dfrac{\cancel{12}\,^{\square} \times 5}{\cancel{8}\,_2}$

$= \dfrac{\square}{\square}$

$= \square\dfrac{\square}{\square}$

b $\dfrac{7}{16} \times 20 = \dfrac{7 \times \cancel{20}^{\,5}}{\cancel{16}}$

$= \dfrac{\square}{\square}$

$= \square\dfrac{\square}{4}$

8 Work out these fractions.

a $\dfrac{9}{16} \times 24$

b $27 \times \dfrac{11}{18}$

c $8 \times \dfrac{9}{20}$

d $30 \times \dfrac{7}{25}$

e $\dfrac{3}{14}$ of 21

f $\dfrac{5}{24}$ of 32

9 $\dfrac{7}{40}$ of the cost of an item is paid as VAT. Calculate the VAT paid on these amounts.

a £60   **b** £20   **c** £24

d £8   **e** £30   **f** £50

10 A grizzly bear may eat up to $\dfrac{3}{20}$ of its body weight in salmon each day. How much salmon do bears of these weights eat?

a 100 kg   **b** 150 kg   **c** 250 kg

*11 Use the formula $F = ma$ to find the value of F.

a $m = 10$ and $a = \dfrac{3}{4}$ **b** $m = 25$ and $a = \dfrac{7}{10}$ **c** $m = \dfrac{2}{3}$ and $a = 60$

*12 Use the formula $v = u + at$ to find v.

a $u = 12$, $a = \dfrac{3}{5}$ and $t = 15$ **b** $u = 3$, $a = \dfrac{7}{8}$ and $t = 20$

c $u = 10$, $a = \dfrac{7}{100}$ and $t = 50$ **d** $u = -1$, $a = 6$ and $t = \dfrac{3}{4}$

Direct proportion

- Recognising direct proportion
- Calculating unknown values using direct proportion
- Exploring the connection between direct proportion and graphs

Keywords

You should know

explanation 1

1 The tables below show pairs of values of x and y.

Which tables show x and y in direct proportion?

a

x	1	2	3
y	3	6	9

b

x	1	2	3
y	7	9	11

c

x	4	12	20
y	2	6	10

d

x	1.5	2	2.5
y	3.5	4	4.5

e

x	10	20	30
y	4	8	12

f

x	50	75	100
y	15	20	25

2 Copy and complete these tables so that x and y are in direct proportion.

a

x	5	7	9
y	10		

b

x	8	9	
y	24		33

c

x	10	18	
y		9	15

d

x	15	21	27
y			9

e

x	7		19
y	3.5	8	

f

x	1.2	1.5	
y		4.5	5.1

explanation 2

3 Rectangles A and B have the same height.

A 80 cm²

B

11.3 cm   22.6 cm

Find the area of rectangle B.

4 Fred is pouring water into his fish
   tank. It takes 18 litres of water to
   fill the tank to a depth of 15 cm.

   a How much water is needed to
      make the depth 5 cm?

   b Fred wants the depth to be
      25 cm.

      How much water will he need in
      the tank?

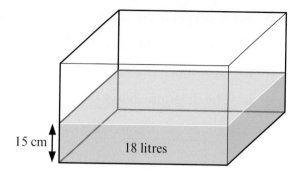

15 cm

18 litres

5 Some instructions for making porridge say that 42 g of porridge oats should be
   mixed with 300 ml of milk.

   a What amount of porridge oats should be mixed with 100 ml of milk?

   b Mrs Brown uses 400 ml of milk to make enough porridge for two small bowls.

      What amount of porridge oats should she use?

6 A regional television company charges advertisers £15 900 for 30 seconds of air
   time in the late evening.

   a How much would it cost for 10 seconds of air time at this rate?

   b An advertiser buys 8 evening spots of 20 seconds. How much does this cost?

   c The cost to advertise across all regions is £45 000 for 30 seconds of air time.

      What is the cost for 8 spots of 20 seconds across all regions?

7 A skip hire company charges the
   amounts shown in the table.

   a Give an example to show
      that the cost to hire is *not*
      proportional to the size of
      the skip.

   b If the cost to hire was
      proportional to the size of the
      skip, how much would it cost for
      the 10 cubic yard skip, based
      on the 2 cubic yard price?

Size (cubic yards)	Cost to hire
2	£125
3	£150
6	£212
8	£250
10	

8 Some carpet is on sale for £52 per square metre.

The carpet is sold from a roll that is 4 m wide.

   a How much does it cost for each metre of carpet from the roll?

   b The diagram shows the measurements of Jenny's lounge.

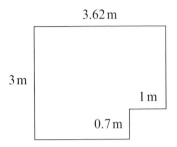

    i What length of carpet must Jenny buy for her lounge?

   ii How much will the carpet cost?

9 Tariq decides to swim a mile at his local swimming pool.

He has to swim 48 lengths of the pool.

He swims 30 lengths in 25 minutes.

How long does Tariq take to swim 48 lengths at this speed?

10 The ingredients for sticky toffee pudding are shown here.

The amounts are based on a recipe for 6 people.

Sticky toffee pudding recipe	
Pudding	**Sauce**
150 g dates	180 g butter
250 ml hot water	360 g brown sugar
60 g butter	250 ml double cream
50 g caster sugar	
2 eggs	
150 g self-raising flour	

   a Work out the amounts needed to serve 3 people.

   b How much brown sugar is needed to make the pudding for 9 people?

   c How much butter is needed to make the pudding for 5 people?

11 a Copy and complete the table below to show that
  s is directly proportional to *t*.

t	0	2	4
s			8

b Copy these axes and plot the values from the table as coordinates.

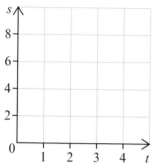

c Join the points with a straight line.

d Write an equation connecting *s* and *t*.

12 a Copy and complete this table for the equation $s = 3t + 2$.

t	0	2	4
s			

b Is *s* directly proportional to *t* in this case?

c Copy these axes and plot the points from your table as coordinates.

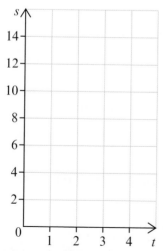

d Join the points with a straight line.

e What difference do you notice between this straight line and the one in
  question **11**?

Deriving expressions and formulae

- Finding expressions and formulae in a variety of situations

Keywords

You should know

explanation 1

1 Write an expression for the number that is

    a 3 more than m **b** 5 less than m **c** twice as big as m

    d half as big as m **e** m more than 7   **f** m less than 11

2 Write an expression for the number that is

    a the product of m and n **b** the sum of m and n **c** m more than n

    d n less than m **e** m less than n **f** m times as big as n

3 n is an odd number. Write an expression for

    a the next odd number   **b** the next even number

    c the previous even number   **d** the previous odd number

4 p is a prime number greater than 2. Write an expression for

    a the next odd number   **b** the previous even number

5 Each card below shows an expression that represents a number.

$n + 2$ $n - 1$ $n + 5$

    a Write the numbers shown on the cards in order, smallest first.

    b What is the median of the numbers?

    c Find and simplify an expression for the sum of the numbers.

    d Factorise your answer to part **c**.

    e Write an expression for the mean of the numbers.

    f What is the range of the numbers?

explanation 2

6 Write an expression for the number midway between each pair of values.

a $n, n + 2$ b $n - 1, n + 1$ c $3n, 3n + 4$

7 The numbers represented by the expressions on these cards are in order, smallest first.

| $t + 2$ | $2t$ | $2t + 6$ | $3t + 4$ |

a   Write an expression for

  i   the median of the numbers   ii   the range of the numbers

  iii   the sum of the numbers   iv   the mean of the numbers

b   What do you notice about the median and the mean?

8 In this diagram, P has coordinates $(a - 2, 3)$.

a   How far is P from the line $x = a$?

b   P' is the image of P after reflection in the line $x = a$.

What are the coordinates of P'?

c   What is the distance PP'?

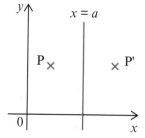

9 Repeat question **8** but take the coordinates of P to be $(1, 5)$.

10 The point Q is mapped to Q' by the translation 3 right and 5 down.

Find the coordinates of Q' when Q is

a $(1, 7)$ b $(x, 3)$ c (x, y)

11 Describe the translation that will map $P(a - 1, b + 2)$ to $P'(a + 3, 2)$.

12 Write a formula for y in terms of x for each of these function machines.

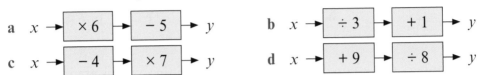

a $x \to \boxed{\times 6} \to \boxed{-5} \to y$

b $x \to \boxed{\div 3} \to \boxed{+1} \to y$

c $x \to \boxed{-4} \to \boxed{\times 7} \to y$

d $x \to \boxed{+9} \to \boxed{\div 8} \to y$

13 To find T, start with n, double it, add 5 and divide the answer by 3.
Write a formula for T in terms of n.

14 To find y, start with x, divide it by 4 and add on 7.
Write a formula for y in terms of x.

15 a Copy and complete this function machine for the formula $y = 3(x + 5)$.

$x \to \boxed{} \to \boxed{} \to y$

b Draw a function machine for the formula $P = 2n - 7$.

c Draw a function machine for the formula $R = \dfrac{d - 6}{10}$.

16 Here are some matchstick patterns.

a How many matchsticks will there be in Pattern 10?

b Write a formula for the number of matchsticks, m, in Pattern n.

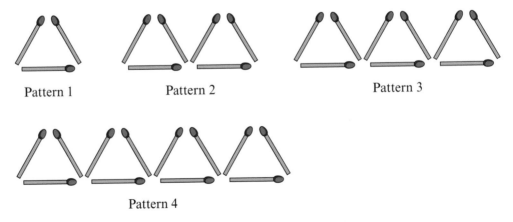

Pattern 1   Pattern 2   Pattern 3

Pattern 4

17 Here are some more matchstick patterns.

Pattern 1   Pattern 2   Pattern 3

Pattern 4

  a Copy and complete the table below.

Pattern number (n)	Number of matchsticks (m)
1	
2	
3	
4	
5	
6	

  b How many matchsticks will there be in Pattern 10?

  c Find a formula for m in terms of n.

  d Which pattern contains 301 matches?

18 a Write down the next two terms of the following sequence.

4, 7, 10, 13, ...

  b What is the tenth term of the sequence?

  c Find a formula for the nth term of the sequence.

19 a Write down the next two terms of the following sequence.

95, 90, 85, 80, ...

  b What is the tenth term of the sequence?

  c Find a formula for the nth term of the sequence.

Using equations

- Using an equation to represent a problem
- Using the solution of the equation to solve the problem

Keywords

You should know

explanation 1a explanation 1b

1 Solve these equations.

   a $n + 11 = 16$ **b** $t - 10 = 45$ **c** $4p = 24$

   d $7z = 35$ **e** $2h + 1 = 17$ **f** $2m - 1 = 11$

2 Solve these equations.

   a $3x + 5 = 38$ **b** $10x - 14 = 56$ **c** $12 + 7x = 54$

   d $48 - 5x = 13$ **e** $22 = 7x - 41$ **f** $87 = 3x + 12$

3 Solve these equations. Give your answers as fractions in their lowest terms.

   a $8p + 11 = 15$ **b** $16 + 9t = 22$ **c** $24 - 10n = 18$

   d $35 = 12a + 27$ **e** $41 = 17y + 29$ **f** $46 + 24g = 61$

4 Solve these equations. Give your answers as mixed numbers.

   a $14 + 5r = 30$ **b** $50 - 8h = 39$ **c** $35 = 7d + 15$

   d $29 = 11x - 24$ **e** $9s - 23 = -4$ **f** $-9 = 4k - 18$

5 Solve these equations. Give your answers as decimals.

   a $9 + 2g = 16$ **b** $25 = 16 + 4w$ **c** $5x + 11 = 14$

   d $-8 + 10b = 81$ **e** $14m + 9 = 30$ **f** $31 - 6y = 4$

6 Simplify and solve these equations.

   a $2x + 7 + 3x - 4 = 33$ **b** $x + (x + 1) + (x + 2) + (x + 3) = 34$

explanation 2

7 You can use algebra to help you solve the puzzle
shown on this scroll.

Use x to represent Lucy's age in years.

a Write an expression for Scott's age using x.

b How old is each of their parents in terms of x?

c Write an expression for the sum of all four ages
and simplify it.

d Use the final piece of information from the
scroll to write an equation.

e Solve the equation.

f How old is Scott?

> **Age-old puzzle**
>
> Scott is 3 years older than
> his sister Lucy.
>
> Their parents are the same
> age, which is three times
> Lucy's age.
>
> The sum of all four ages is
> 99 years. How old is Scott?

8

> This diagram shows an addition pyramid.
>
> The bottom three numbers are
> consecutive integers, increasing from left
> to right.
>
> What are the missing numbers?

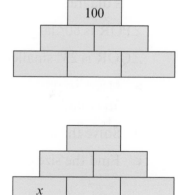

Follow the steps below to solve the puzzle.

a Copy the second diagram and write expressions
for the missing numbers in the bottom row.

b Use the rules for an addition pyramid to find
expressions for the other missing numbers.

Simplify them and write them in the spaces.

c Write an equation using what you know about the top number in the
pyramid.

d Solve the equation.

e Copy the top diagram and fill in the missing numbers.

9 Karam added 5 consecutive integers to make a total of 2010.

What were the integers that Karam used?

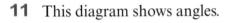

> Use *x* to represent the first number.

10 In this triangle

$\angle ACB = 2 \times \angle ABC$

$\angle BAC = \angle ABC + \angle ACB$

  a Use *x* to represent $\angle ABC$ and write

   i $\angle ACB$ in terms of *x*

   ii $\angle BAC$ in terms of *x*

   iii an equation based on the sum of the angles

  b Solve the equation.

  c Find the size of each angle.

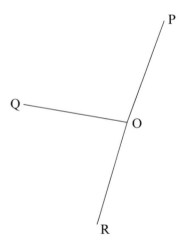

11 This diagram shows angles.

$\angle POR$ is 80° larger than $\angle POQ$

$\angle QOR$ is 23° smaller than $\angle POQ$

  a Use *x* to represent $\angle POQ$ and write an equation based on the sum of the angles.

  b Solve the equation.

  c Find the size of each angle.

explanation 3

12 Solve these equations.

  a $3(x + 11) = 48$ **b** $4(x - 9) = 24$ **c** $6(12 - x) = 18$

  d $8(3 + x) = 72$ **e** $6(x + 8) = 30$ **f** $5(3 - x) = 35$

13 Solve these equations by expanding the brackets first.

    a $4(h + 2.5) = 30$ **b** $5(r + 2) + 11 = 56$ **c** $42 = 4(d - 1) + 6$

    d $34 = g + 4(2g - 5)$ **e** $p + 3(p - 7) = 23$ **f** $9(v + 1) - 2v - 44 = 0$

14 Solve these equations.

    a $\dfrac{x + 11}{4} = 7$ **b** $\dfrac{u}{5} - 9 = 2$ **c** $14 = \dfrac{t + 23}{3}$

    d $\dfrac{y}{10} + 19 = 23$ **e** $\dfrac{a - 7}{6} = 5$ **f** $-7 = \dfrac{e}{5} - 11$

15 **a** Write an expression for the area of triangle ABC.

    b The area of the triangle is $30\,\text{cm}^2$.

        Write this information as an equation.

    c Solve the equation.

    d Write down the length of AC.

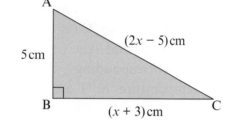

16 **a** I think of a number, add 17 and then divide by 5. My answer is 5.4.

        Write this information as an equation. Solve the equation to find my number.

    b I think of a number, divide it by 6, then subtract the result from 20. My answer is 11.5.

        Write this information as an equation. Solve the equation to find my number.

17 The nth term of a sequence is $4(n + 9)$.

    a Which term has value 96?

    b How many terms have a value less than 50?

    c Show that there isn't a term with value 45.

18 Find the coordinates of the point where the graph of $y = \dfrac{x + 7}{3}$ crosses the graph of $y = 4$.

Graphs of real-life situations

• Interpreting the information shown by a graph

explanation 1

1 This graph shows oven
temperatures between
130 °C and 240 °C on
the horizontal axis.
The corresponding
temperatures in °F are
shown on the vertical axis.

a Use the graph
to convert these
temperatures to
Fahrenheit.

   i 135 °C

   ii 180 °C

   iii 210 °C

b Use the graph
to convert these
temperatures to
Celsius.

   i 320 °F

   ii 392 °F

   iii 437 °F

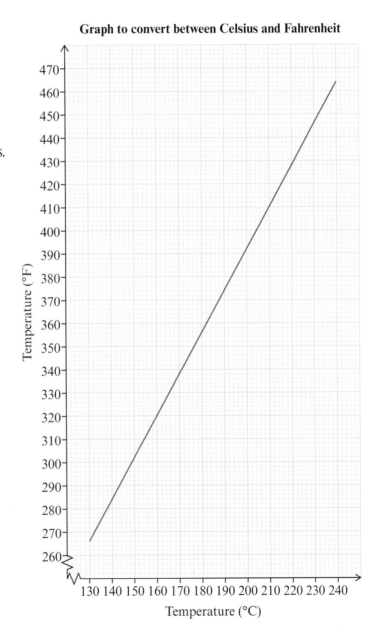

Graph to convert between Celsius and Fahrenheit

2 1000 miles is the same as 1600 kilometres.

a **i** How many kilometres are there in 100 miles?

ii How many kilometres are there in 500 miles?

iii How many kilometres are there in 800 miles?

b Copy this diagram onto graph paper.

i Plot a point on the diagram to show that 1000 miles is the same as 1600 km.

ii Use your answers to parts **a ii** and **a iii** to plot two more points on your diagram.

iii Draw a straight line through the three points.

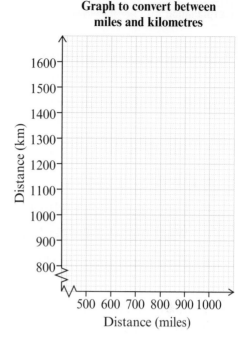

Graph to convert between miles and kilometres

c Use your graph to convert these distances to kilometres.

i 550 miles   **ii** 720 miles   **iii** 960 miles

d Use your graph to convert these distances to miles.

i 960 km   **ii** 1040 km   **iii** 1360 km

3 **a** Draw and label a pair of axes and plot points to show the information in the table.

Inches	24	36	60
Millimetres	600	900	1500

b Draw a straight line graph through your plotted points.

c Use your graph to convert these distances to millimetres.

i 32 inches   **ii** 41 inches   **iii** 53 inches

d Use your graph to convert these distances to inches.

i 925 millimetres   **ii** 1100 millimetres   **iii** 1225 millimetres

explanation 2

4 Mira set off from home to take a walk. This graph shows her progress.

a Mira stopped for a rest. What time did she stop?

b How long did she rest for?

c How far did she walk altogether?

d How long did her return journey take?

e What time did she get home?

f How much time did she spend walking?

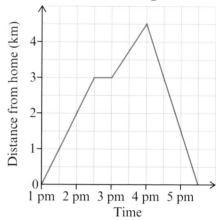

Graph showing distance from home during a walk

5 Callum and Alex raced each other over two lengths of a swimming pool. This graph shows what happened.

a Who turned first?

b How long was the pool?

c What distance was left to go when they were level with each other?

d Who won the race?

e What did Alex do that was different to Callum?

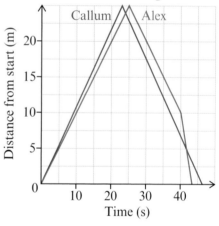

Graph showing distance from start during race

6 A ball is dropped onto a hard surface. This graph shows how its height changes with time up to the fourth bounce.

a From what height was the ball dropped?

b How long did it take to reach the ground?

c How high did the ball reach on its first bounce?

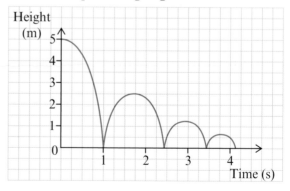

Graph showing height of bounce

d On which bounce did the ball reach less than 1 m for the first time?

explanation 3 ─────────────────────────

7 This graph shows the speed of a
rollercoaster during the first 50 seconds
of a ride.

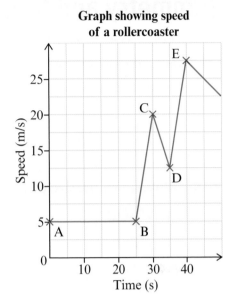

Graph showing speed
of a rollercoaster

a What can you say about the speed
corresponding to the first section AB
of the graph?

b Which point on the rollercoaster do
you think B corresponds to?

c Describe what section BC shows.

d Describe what section CD shows.

e What is the greatest speed shown on
the graph?

8 A firework rocket is pointed vertically upwards. This graph shows how the
speed of the rocket changes with time.

Graph showing speed of a firework rocket

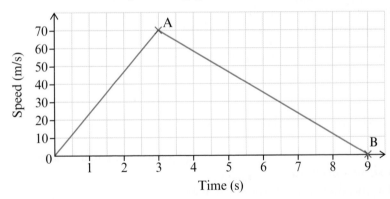

a Describe what is happening to the rocket during the first 3 seconds of its
flight.

b What is the greatest speed of the rocket?

c Describe what the section AB of the graph represents.

d Which of the labelled points corresponds to the greatest height reached?
Explain your answer.

Symmetry and transformations

- Exploring rotational symmetry
- Investigating the connection between line symmetry and reflection
- Exploring the combined effect of reflection and translation

Keywords

You should know

explanation 1a   explanation 1b   explanation 1c

1 a Write down the size of these angles.

  i ∠AOB

  ii ∠BOC

  iii ∠AOC

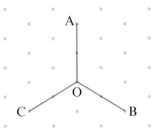

  b The figure is now rotated through an obtuse angle about O to the position shown.

  i What is the angle and direction of rotation?

  ii If the rotation is repeated twice more, what can you say about the final position of the figure?

  iii What is the order of rotational symmetry of the figure?

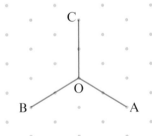

2 Points A, B and C of the diagram in question **1** are joined to make a triangle.

  a What type of triangle is this?

  b What is the order of rotational symmetry of the triangle?

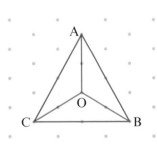

3 The shape shown here is a regular pentagon.

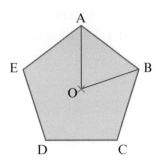

  a Explain why ∠AOB must be 72°.

  b The pentagon is rotated through 72° clockwise about O. Sketch the pentagon in this position.

  c How many more of these rotations are needed to return the pentagon to its original position?

  d Write down the order of rotational symmetry of a regular pentagon.

4 This shape is a regular octagon.

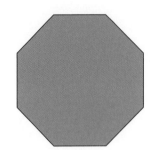

  a The octagon is rotated about its centre so that it maps onto itself. What is the smallest angle for this rotation?

  b How many more of these rotations are needed to return the octagon to its original position?

  c What is the order of rotational symmetry of a regular octagon?

5 Write down the order of rotational symmetry of each shape.

a

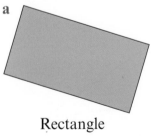

Rectangle

b

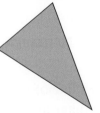

Isosceles triangle

c

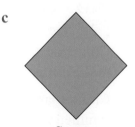

Square

d

Parallelogram

e

Trapezium

f

Hexagon

6 Copy and complete these diagrams so that they have rotational symmetry of order 4 with centre at O.

a

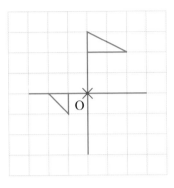

b

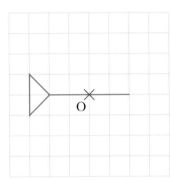

c

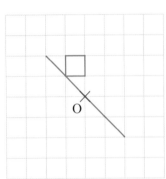

d

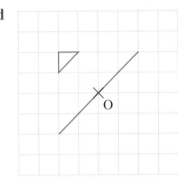

explanation 2

7 a Copy this diagram and reflect the triangle in the dotted line.

   b Check that the dotted line is a line of symmetry for the completed diagram.

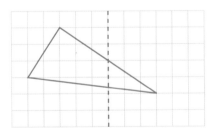

8 a Copy this diagram and reflect the arrowhead in the dotted line.

   b Check that the dotted line is a line of symmetry for the completed diagram.

   c Add any other lines of symmetry to the diagram.

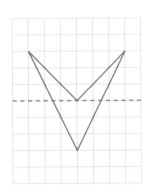

9 a   Copy this diagram and reflect the shape in the dotted line.

b   Check that the dotted line is a line of symmetry for the completed diagram.

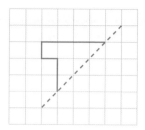

10 Copy these shapes and draw any lines of symmetry. If no line of symmetry exists then write 'None'.

a

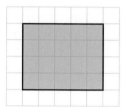

b

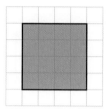

c

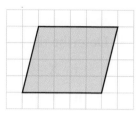

d

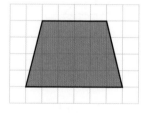

e

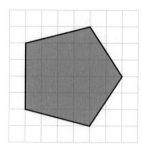

f

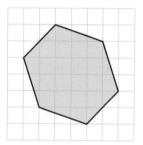

11 For each shape, state which of these symmetries it has.

A   Line symmetry but not rotational symmetry.
B   Rotational symmetry but not line symmetry.
C   Both rotational symmetry and line symmetry.

a

b

c

d

e

f

explanation 3

12 Describe each translation.

    a A to B   **b** C to A

    c D to C   **d** B to D

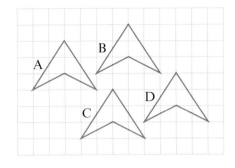

13 Describe these translations.

    i X → Y

    ii Y → Z

    iii X → Z

  b Shape Y maps to shape P by the translation '7 right and 2 up'. Describe the translation X → P.

  c Shape Y maps to shape Q by the translation '4 down'.

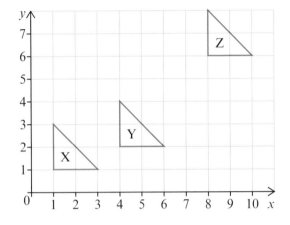

    i Copy and complete. Translation Y → Q is ☐ right and ☐ up.

    ii Describe translation X → Q.

14 The pattern shown in the diagram continues forever in both directions.

  a Which of these translations will map the whole pattern onto itself?

    i 2 right   **ii** 4 right

    iii 8 left   **iv** 3 left

    v 1000 right   **vi** 4*n* right where *n* is an integer

  b Describe a reflection, followed by a translation that maps the whole pattern onto itself.

  c Describe a translation followed by a reflection that maps the whole pattern onto itself.

Solving geometrical problems

- Applying your knowledge to solve problems

Keywords

You should know

explanation 1

1 You have this rectangle and these two right-angled triangles.

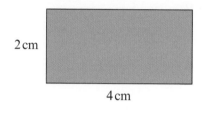 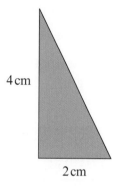 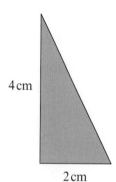

You can translate, rotate or reflect any of the shapes and combine them to build new shapes.

Draw diagrams to show how to build these shapes.

a A square

b Two different parallelograms

c Two different trapeziums

d Two different isosceles triangles

e A pentagon

2 a Show that this diagram contains two isosceles triangles.

b Calculate the distance AD.

Explain your method.

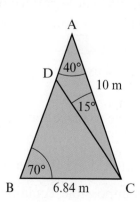

207

3 In this diagram, ABCD is a rectangle.

The blue arc is a quarter of a circle with centre at D.

Find the length of AC and explain your reasoning.

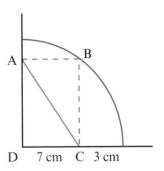

D   7 cm   C 3 cm

4 A spider is about to walk from A to B on the surface of the cube. Each side of the cube is 5 cm long.

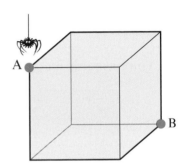

a The spider takes the shortest path from A to B.

How long is this path to the nearest 0.1 cm?

b How many different paths are there between A and B that have this length?

5 a Find the number of squares in each of these diagrams.

Count squares of different sizes and look for a pattern.

i   ii   iii   iv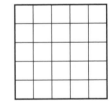

b How many squares are there on a chessboard?

6 This diagram shows a chessboard pattern with a pair of opposite corners removed.

You are given 31 domino-shaped tiles like this one shown here.

Each tile will exactly cover two squares of the chessboard.

Is it possible to place the tiles on the chessboard pattern so that it is completely covered?

- If it can be done, draw a diagram to show how.

- If it is impossible, ecplain why.

7 The diagram shows a cube made from 27 smaller cubes that have been stuck together. Individual cubes are easily removed.

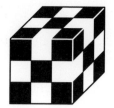

- Choose any outside cube as a starting point and remove it.

- Now choose a cube that was next to the one removed. Remove it.

- Continue in this way until there is just one cube left.

Is it possible to do this so that the last cube is the one in the centre?

8 This diagram represents two towns A and B with a canal running between them.

A bridge is to be built across the canal at right angles to the banks so that the road needed to link the two towns is as short as possible.

Copy the diagram and show the best position for the bridge. Explain your reasoning.

A ✕

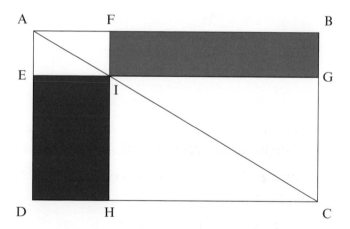

B ✕

9 This diagram shows a large rectangle with red and blue rectangles drawn inside.

Which of these statements is true?

- The blue area is greater than the red area.

- The red area is greater than the blue area.

- The blue and red areas are equal.

Explain your reasoning.